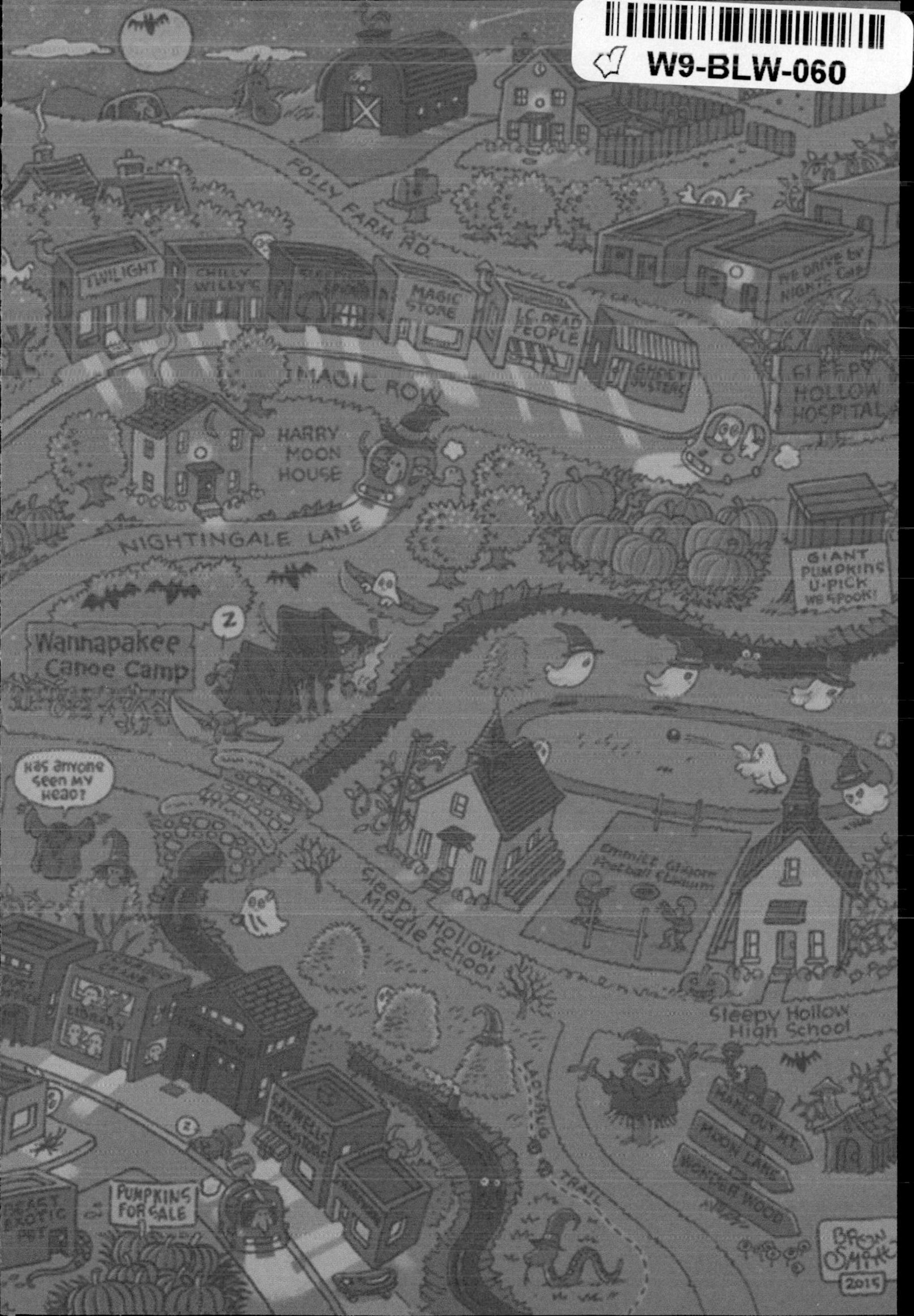
FOLLY FARM RD.
TWILIGHT
CHILLY WILLY'S
MAGIC STORE
I.C. DEAD PEOPLE
MAGIC ROW
SLEEPY HOLLOW HOSPITAL
HARRY MOON HOUSE
NIGHTINGALE LANE
GIANT PUMPKINS U-PICK WE SPOOK!
Wannapakee Canoe Camp
Has anyone seen my head?
Sleepy Hollow Middle School
Sleepy Hollow High School
LIBRARY
MAKE-OUT MT.
MOON LANE
WONDER WOOD
TRAIL
PUMPKINS FOR SALE
2015

The

AMAZING

ADVENTURES OF

HARRY MOON

TIME MACHINE

by
Mark Andrew Poe

Illustrations by Christina Weidman

rabbit publishers

Time Machine (The Amazing Adventures of Harry Moon,
by Mark Andrew Poe

Rabbit Publishers
1624 W. Northwest Highway
Arlington Heights, IL 60004

Illustrations by Christina Weidman
Cover Design by Chris D'Antonio
Interior Design by Lewis Design & Marketing
Creative Consultants: David Kirkpatrick, Thom Black and Paul Lewis

ISBN: 978-1-943785-04-9

10 9 8 7 6 5 4 3 2 1

1. Fiction - Action and Adventure 2. Children's Fiction
First Edition
Printed in U.S.A.

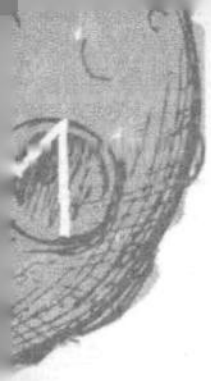

"I am on to you."

~ RABBIT

TABLE OF CONTENTS

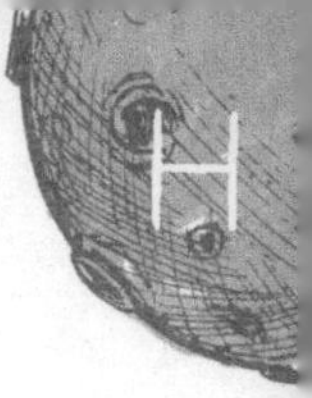
H

PREFACE

Halloween visited the little town of Sleepy Hollow and never left.

Many moons ago, a sly and evil mayor found the powers of darkness helpful in building Sleepy Hollow into "Spooky Town," one of the country's most celebrated attractions. Now, years later, a young eighth grade magician, Harry Moon, is chosen by the powers of light to do battle against the mayor and his evil consorts.

Welcome to *The Amazing Adventures of Harry Moon*. Darkness may have found a home in Sleepy Hollow, but if young Harry has anything to say about it, darkness will not be staying.

THE SHORT KID

It was tough enough being the shortest kid in the eighth grade. Harry Moon did not need to be reminded that he was that kid.

Titus Kligore slammed into Harry walking down the corridor to third period Geography at Sleepy Hollow Middle School, splattering

Harry up against the lockers. "What's up with you being so short, anyways?" Titus asked. He squeezed his eyes small as he looked down at Harry, flicking Harry's inky black hair with his long index finger.

"Knock it off, Titus. Don't you ever get tired of being a jerk?" Harry pushed Titus's arm away.

"What's the answer, little guy? Why are you a Lilliputian? Your dad is normal size and so is your mom. What happened to you?"

"I just came this way," Harry said.

"Maybe so, runt-bod. But seriously, Bro, are you ever gonna get over it?" Titus stared down at Harry's curly head.

"You mean like the flu?"

"Yeah, like the swine I-have-a-tiny-little-butt flu." Titus laughed out loud at his own words.

"Only time will tell." Harry sighed and looked down the crowded hallway. Yep, he was

definitely the shortest kid in *this* school.

3

"Yeah, but don't feel SO bad. You're different. You *know stuff*. So, why don't you gaze into your crystal ball and see if you're always gonna stay a runt."

"I don't have a crystal ball," Harry Moon said. "I have a wand."

"Then, just do it, Dude. We all know you have the magic. Just do your Abracadabra *thang*. You can do it. I know you can. Make yourself big, magic man." Titus tousled Harry's hair.

"Lay off. It doesn't work that way."

"What way? Come on, you are the king around here. You are even better than Elvis Gold. You rule," Titus said. "Man, if you were tall, you might even be able to steal another kiss from Sarah Sinclair."

"Doubtful, Einstein," said Harry. "And that kiss wasn't stolen." But Harry kind of thought Titus might be right. *Maybe if I were taller, I could get Sarah Sinclair to love me.*

Harry's first and only kiss with Sarah Sinclair only happened because Harry stood on an apple crate. Otherwise, their lips would never have met. Harry knew that someday things might change. His doctor said that he would grow taller. And he wasn't *Ripley's Believe It Or Not* short. He was just short enough not to be tall.

With a final nod, Harry sized up his friend and foe, Titus Kligore. For all his bluster, he was one big guy.

"I'm going to try a few things when I get home from school," Harry said, looking up at Titus. "I might just have a few tricks up my sleeve."

"Alright," said Titus. "Now you're talking *your* language. That's what I want to hear."

Titus gave Harry a quick shoulder punch, sending him stumbling into the lockers again and walked into his third period Geo class.

"Thanks, Titus." Harry pulled himself up off the floor.

Titus looked back at Harry. "Thanks for what?"

"The pep talk," Harry said.

"Always ready to brighten your day, little man. Now, get on it," Titus said. "Get on your magic."

BIG BLUE BIKE

eavenly Bamboo is a member of the barberry family of plants. It's not actually related to bamboo. It is a suckering evergreen shrub. Heavenly Bamboo grows easily and quickly, similar to regular bamboo. It can grow from a seedling to eight feet in just one season.

It was an essential element in the growth spell that Harry Moon found in his *Gri-*

moire, a Book of Spells. The word Grimoire was taken from the word 'grammar' and was sort of a 'how to' on magic. Samson Dupree, Harry's mentor and also the eccentric, mysterious proprietor of the Sleepy Hollow Magic Shop gave Harry the Grimoire for his thirteenth birthday.

Samson wore strange clothes like red velvet slippers instead of shoes. He was a bit of a performer, too. In the Magic Shop, Samson Dupree wore a magician's cape and a plastic, golden crown. "I don't need real gold," Samson had said, "I just like the color."

Harry appreciated Samson. They connected in a very special way and he knew tons of magic. Samson was great at everything including the one arm vanish. That's where you drop your caped arm and whatever was behind you, vanishes into thin air.

"Why does the book say, 'Be warned'?" Harry had asked when he opened his birthday gift from Samson that summer. The book was bound in brown leather etched with odd runes and symbols. Harry figured it must be as old as

the hills surrounding Sleepy Hollow.

"The Source of all magic is never ending," said Samson. "Magic can be used for good or evil. But the Greatest Magician of all desires for you to use your powers for good."

Harry sat on the vinyl-covered, wobbly stool near the counter. "But why does it say, 'Be Warned' Samson?"

"Because a book like this could get into the wrong hands. Those words, 'Be Warned' help scare the confused away."

"The confused?" Harry asked. "Who are the confused?" He touched the words BE WARNED and a slight tingle of excitement ran up his arm.

Samson took a deep breath. What he had to say was important. "When someone doesn't know what they want and are confused about right and wrong and uses a book like this, well, they could create a lot of trouble."

"The wonderful and scary thing about life is that we are given free choice about such things. Never use magic, Harry, if you find yourself confused and aren't sure which way is up. That's just chaos."

Harry breathed deeply. "I am thirteen years old," he said. "*I AM* ready for this."

Samson studied Harry's face. "Use this book wisely, then. Think not only with your mind but your heart. Don't be a flibbertigibbet." Samson smiled with a nod.

"Huh?"

"A flibbertigibbet. Flighty. A flibbertigibbet is someone who flits around from one thing to the next. Take a stand. Be strong and courageous," said Samson as he adjusted his plastic crown on his stacked hair. He reached out and picked a ladybug off Harry's shoulder and set it on the counter. "Mmmm. Must have come in with you. Off with you."

Harry ran his fingers over the words BE

WARNED again. "That's a tall order, Samson."

"That's what being tall is all about, Harry. Just like the chivalrous knights of King Arthur's court. They were virtuous." Samson adjusted his cape. "Aim for those magical words that your mom has stenciled on the kitchen wall — *love, patience, goodness* — there is something to them."

Harry screwed up his face. "Wait a sec. You've been to Mom's kitchen?"

"I do know of it, yes," answered Samson with a hint of a smile. "I am a magician, am I not?"

Harry stared at Samson and wondered. There was definitely something strange about the guy. He'd never admit to being anything other than an old man and a magician. But Harry knew something was up. Whenever Harry asked him if he was an angel, an archangel, or some other kind of heavenly being not yet revealed, Samson blew off Harry's questions with a wave of his hand

and a smile. But not just an ordinary smile. No, Samson's smiles were full of deep kindness that nevertheless said, "Mind your own business, kiddo."

Samson Dupree turned the Grimoire to face him. He flipped through pages lavishly illustrated with engravings of herbs, stones, fancy contraptions, light and even darkness. Samson stopped on a page with a beautiful and large Harlequin Rabbit.

"Hey, look at that," Harry said. "That's a picture of Rabbit." Rabbit was a friend Samson had given Harry on the day of the annual Sleepy Hollow Middle School Talent Show. He was a very large, Harlequin Rabbit that only Harry could see and talk to.

"Rabbit makes it into all the books," said Samson. This time Samson's eyes seemed even deeper and more mysterious. Harry had to fight the urge to ask more questions. He knew Samson would only smile and wave them away like mosquitoes. So Harry said the only thing he could, "Thanks, Samson! This is so cool!"

And he meant it. In fact Harry was so excited that he practically spun around on the stool.

"There will always be trouble in the world, Harry," Samson Dupree had said. "So there will always be a need for champions of right and wrong." Samson closed the book and placed it in Harry's hands. "Remember, Harry, each and every one of us has an important story. Only a few will become heroes."

Harry swallowed. *Hero? Me?*

13

Not only did the Growth Spell require two cups of ground Heavenly Bamboo, but also required the flowers of the mandrake plant and a broken shell from a robin's egg.

The ingredients were to be crushed in a mortar with a pestle, then blended with fresh spring water. Harry was able to purchase the roots and flowers on eBay. He even found the broken eggshell under the tree in his front yard. The only thing missing was the fresh spring water. Harry figured the word "fresh" was important.

Harry and his friend Hao Jones were eating lunch together at school. Today's cafeteria pizza and shriveled tater tots was being served with a fruit cup that looked more like a big-chunk vomit cup.

"Barf," muttered Harry as he dug his spoon into the smushed up pineapples and bananas. "This smells absolutely gross." He leaned away from the table and gagged.

"Hey, forget that. Here, use this for your growing thing," said Hao as he pulled a plastic bottle from his backpack. "Look at the label. Spring water."

"That could be false advertising," said Harry. "I bet it's from a hose. And besides the recipe calls for FRESH water. I know a spring right off Folly Farm Road. I prefer to know my source."

"All right, then," Hao said. "Let's go."

"Agreed," Harry said. "Right after school, out front, bikes. Be there."

The instant the final bell rang, Harry and Hao ran down the front steps of Sleepy Hollow Middle School, jumped on their bikes and wound their way through Sleepy Hollow out into the country. Sure enough, in the white birch forest at the edge of Folly Farm, there was a bubbling pool. Because it was a gurgler, the water was always churning, remaining free from algae. The water was crystal clear.

15

"Huh. I didn't know this was here. This is great!" said Hao. He got on his knees and unscrewed the cap on his empty water bottle from Sleepy Hollow Outfitters. With just a few dunks, Hao filled the bottle with pure, fresh H-2-O. "I am one fine sorcerer's apprentice," he said, holding up the bottle to the sun and letting the light fool with the water. "Makes me thirsty."

Harry pulled the zipper on his backpack. He reached inside and removed a Ziploc bag holding the ground-up Growth Spell ingredients: one cracked robin's egg, mandrake flowers and Heavenly Bamboo. "Here goes nothing," he said and sprinkled the mixture into the bottle. He screwed on the cap tight, took a deep breath and shook the bottle.

"Now what?" asked Hao. He was leaning against a birch tree, wondering if he should bother retying his shoe or just let it flop around untied. Why bother tying shoes if they kept coming untied? "Are you 'sposed to drink this growth stuff? I bet it tastes like dirty socks."

"No way," Harry said. "Yuck. The Grimoire says once I say, "Abracadabra," I'm supposed to sprinkle it on the object that I want to grow."

"Object? Hold on, Harry dude. You're not an *object*," said Hao, "You're a *kid*. A person. Does it say this growing thing works on people?"

"Mmmm," Harry said, confused. "Let me think about this. I better check the book. Here, hold the bottle and don't spill any." Harry handed Hao the water bottle and pulled the Grimoire from his backpack. "Let's see what it says about this."

"Good idea," said Hao.

"Better be sure it works on people." Harry put the leather-bound Grimoire on the ground and opened to the page with the growth spell recipe. "I have to get this right. You can't mess around with magic. And..." he said remembering Samson's words, "one ought not reach out with magic when confused."

"What does it say?" Hao asked.

"Mmmm, you're right," Harry said, running his finger over the text. "It does say here *object*. Not people."

"This is one of those be *careful what you wish for* stories!" said Hao.

"What do you mean?" Harry asked. He stood and brushed his knees of the leaves and dirt. He shook the Grimoire and blew the dirt from the cover.

"You know, *careful what you wish for,*" Hao said. "You sprinkle that stuff on you and POOF! You become a ten-foot tall giant. You're big, alright. So big, that they come and hunt you down in helicopters with rapid fire guns and kill you like King Kong on the Empire State Building cause you are a threat to humanity."

"Thanks. I appreciate that, pal. You've been reading too many comic books, Hao," said Harry.

"Yeah, but NOT LIKE the movies and unlike Marvel comics, this is real. It's not make-believe."

"Just give me the water bottle," said Harry.

"Nope, I can't," said Hao. He held it behind his back. "What if something bad happens, Harry? You get too big and we can't shrink you down and suddenly you are walking around with thighs the size of tree trunks and your head's as big as a garbage truck."

"Come on, don't be ridiculous, bro," Harry said as he grabbed Hao's arm and wrestled the bottle out of his hand.

Harry unscrewed the bottle and held its open mouth over his head, grimacing a little at Hao. "It's time to get taller."

"Don't do it, Moon!" Hao swatted the bottle from Harry's hand. The bottle and its contents went flying into the air.

"Hey, come on! What are you doing! Who's the magician around here anyway?" hollered Harry. "Dontcha think I know what I'm doing, Hao?!"

But just as the words left his mouth, Harry blinked. His eyes went big. The water rained over his bicycle. As fast as the water fell, the blue bicycle with the 21-inch wheels grew ... and grew.

Sprong! The handlebars expanded to the wingspan of a 727. The wheels rose into the sky like a tower.

"Oh no," said Harry as his eyes lifted upward. His blue bicycle touched the top of the tallest oak on Folly Farm. It had to be twenty feet tall. A squirrel leaped from a nearby elm, thinking the bell on the handlebar was one beautiful walnut yet to be cracked. *Ring!* went the bell.

"See what you did, dumb-face!" Harry shouted at his friend.

"Dumb face? That coulda been you, my man! I just saved you from a sad life of gigs with Cirque Du Soleil!"

"I would not have sprinkled the WHOLE BOTTLE on me!"

"You're not a thing, Harry! You're not an object! You are a carefully constructed human being! This magic is not for people!" said Hao.

Harry sat down on the grass next to the spring and looked up at the bike. He wiped his brow.

"You're right, Hao. That was definitely a big save," said Harry. "I owe you. I just want to be tall so much." He hung his head between his knees in the shadow of the huge bicycle seat.
"It's alright, said Hao looking from the giant handlebars to his friend. Against the colossal bike, Harry had managed to appear even

punier. "I get it, Bro."

"Now, what do we do?" Harry asked.

"Maybe we could make a deal with Cirque De Soliel to buy it?" asked Hao. "Seriously, we could make some real *ca-ching*."

"We have to do something with this bike. We probably need for it to disappear," said Harry, "before some droid zooms in and makes a video that will go viral in seconds." Sleepy Hollow already has a headless horseman. It doesn't need a giant bicycle . . . "

". . . or for that matter an alien invasion. Those visitors from Saturn are supposed to be quite large," replied Hao.

"Too much Marvel, man," said Harry.

"You know what I'm going to do, Harry?" Hao sat next to his friend on the grass.
"What?"

"I'm going to put away my comics. Why do

I need Marvel, when I have you?" Hao said, putting his arm on Harry's shoulders.

"Friends?" Hao asked.

"Always. Friends," Harry said.

They both stared at the gargantuan bicycle. "How are we ever gonna hide this . . . this monstrosity?"

"There must be an antidote for the growth spell in your Grimoire," said Hao. "Don't you remember that movie? *Honey I Shrunk the Kids?*"

"But that was a laser gun or something," Harry said. "Not a spell."

"Still," Hao said. "There's got to be a solution."

"I guess I better find it pretty quick," Harry said.

24

TABLE TRICKS

What kind of idiotic thing have you been up to now, *brother?*" asked Honey Moon as she spooned some string beans and almonds from the casserole dish onto her plate. Harry's little sister was sitting at the dining room table with Harry and their parents, Mary Moon and John Moon. Harvest Moon, the baby of the family, was making castles with his applesauce and raisins on his high chair tray.

Harry frowned without looking up. "I don't report my business to an annoying know-it-all like you," said Harry as he bit into his turkey burger slathered in ketchup and mayo.

"You don't need to report anything when you wear your stupid on your back!" Honey said. "Everyone can see it. It's all right there!"

Honey Moon lifted her nose in the air as if a skunk had just sprayed the room.

"Leave your brother alone, Honey, let him eat in peace," said Mary Moon. "And Harry, don't call your sister annoying."

"Yeah! Leave me alone," echoed Harry.

"But, Daddy," Honey Moon said. She turned and smiled at her father. The silver from her braces was bright in the setting sun that filtered through the window. "Don't you want to know why Harry turned that beautiful backpack you bought him at Sleepy Hollow Outfitters into a man purse?"

Harry stopped mid-chew and froze. He wiggled his shoulders and realized his backpack seemed very light. Something was terribly wrong.

"Its NOT a man purse!" he said, as he reached behind him, straining with his fingertips to snag his backpack that he now couldn't seem to reach. The backpack had shrunk in size and he couldn't get at it. Harry shoved his chair away from the table with a kick and stood up. Half Moon, the dog who had been dozing under the table, let go a yelp because Harry accidentally kicked him.

"Dad, can you help me here?" Harry said as he pulled at the backpack's shoulder harness straining against his shoulders. "I can't seem to be able to get this thing off my back. Its too tight."

"Harry, what happened to this thing?" asked John Moon when he saw the tiny, black and yellow backpack strapped to Harry's back.

The backpack had shrunk to the size of a *Lunchable.*

John Moon pulled the tiny, little pack off Harry's back. He let it dangle from his pinky. "What in the world is this? Is this your backpack?"

"Oh no!" said Harry as he looked at the backpack, in pee-wee size, hanging from his Dad's finger like a tiny, tiny toy.

28

John Moon shook his head and handed the pack to Harry. "I don't get it. How did this happen?" asked Harry's dad.

Harry was barely able to find the minuscule zipper. With just his thumb and index finger he pulled out his now tiny schoolbooks and his Grimoire. Tears welled in his eyes as he stared at the ant-sized books in the palm of his hand.

"What's going on?" asked Mary Moon. She gazed into her son's wide eyes. "Don't lie to us, Harry. We can deal with whatever it is as long as it's the truth. Why is everything so small?"

Harry's eyes narrowed and darted to Honey Moon who was always busting his chops for something. His stomach wobbled as he waited for her to say something sarcastic.

Sensing her son's frustration, Mary Moon reached out and took Honey's hand. "And you, young lady, are to say nothing. ABSOLUTELY nothing. Do you understand?"

"Yes, Mom," said Honey. But then she grinned mischievously through her silver grill. "I'll do what I always do: WATCH, LISTEN, and LEARN as to how you discipline your wayward son."

"That's my girl," said Mary Moon, patting her daughter's hand. Then she gave Honey's hand a little squeeze just for emphasis.

Holding back his tears Harry sat down and put his head in his hands. He had no idea how to un-shrink his books. Especially the Grimoire. How could he ever use it to fix his problems?

Harry told his parents the whole mess — wanting to be bigger, the spells, the gigantic bike, and then having to shrink everything small again. "I guess after I got my bike back to normal size, the left-over SHRINKING magic potion must have splashed out onto my back and backpack when I was riding home. And now everything is soooo small."

"Harry, Harry," said Mary Moon. "This is nothing to fool with. This is magic."

Harry rested his head in his hands again. He let go a huge sigh and then looked back at his Dad and Mom. "I know."

Mary Moon patted her son's hand. "This is what we keep talking about, Harry. You have to be careful with the magic," she said. "You must treat your gifts responsibly."

"I know, Mom. I . . . I just am so glad Hao was there. He really saved my butt."

Honey spit milk across the table. "HAO?" she said. "What a loser!"

"Honey, stop," said John Moon. "We don't talk like that."

"What? You said I could only NOT talk about Harry! Doesn't a ten-year-old have any rights around here?"

"Nope. None. Nope." Harry replied sharply.

"Yes, of course you do, Honey," said Mary. "But when we are discussing Harry, you must watch, listen and learn."

"What can I possibly learn from that nerd?" Honey Moon said, her cheeks flushed red like a Macintosh apple. Honey stood from the table. "I shall like to go to my room. Mother, may I be excused?"

"Yes, you may, dear. I think that's a good idea." Honey beat it out of the dining room, muttering to herself. But first she reached under the table and dragged the lazy hound out. "Come on, Half Moon. You're coming with me."

John Moon turned to Harry. He had just finished his second turkey burger and was on to his second helping of home-made sweet potato fries.

"Harry," said John Moon calmly. "I want you to know that there are plenty of people who are . . . er . . . shorter. People who have lived successful, even famous lives," said John Moon.

"Like Napoleon, for example," said Mary Moon, attempting to be helpful.

"He was a tyrant who acted out because he was such a shrimp and hated it," said Harry. "And he killed a bunch of people because of it. Besides, he wasn't really small. He was normal height for people back then. He just felt small."

"Good point, son," said John Moon. "But take film star, Mickey Rooney, for eight decades he worked despite his . . . er . . . diminutive size."

"Yeah, yeah," Harry said. "I read about him too. Before he died, he said his fire-hydrant size limited what he could do on screen."

Harry swiped one of Dad's fries. "Mickey Rooney was never more than somebody's sidekick. He never got the girl."

"But look at Tom Cruise! He is only 5'2" and he always gets the girl!" said Mary Moon.

"That's because he is always standing on an apple crate!" replied Harry. "Been there, done that. I really do NOT want to go through life carrying an apple crate, thank you very much." For a second his thoughts turned to Sarah Sinclair and their first kiss. It was amazing, but still . . . he was perched on an apple crate.

33

He looked over at his parents. His mother's eyes were filled with concern. His dad looked stricken like the Patriots had just lost the Superbowl in overtime. Harry really did love his parents, he really did. He knew they meant well.

"Listen you guys," said Harry, "I am NOT trying to be goofy here. I know you love me. I do. But all I need is to look over at that wall to know that I have a situation."

John Moon glanced across the dining room into the kitchen where Harry was pointing.

"Huh?" asked John. "What are you talking about, Harry?"

Mary Moon looked over at Harry. She had compassion in her eyes. "I know what he's talking about," she said.

Harry stood. While Harvest Moon continued to make castles on the tray, Harry walked across the carpeted floor of the dining room to the kitchen.

Harry pointed to the growth chart that had been penciled into the wood of the threshold since he was two-years-old.

"Here I am at three," said Harry as he point-ed to the 35-inch mark. "Here I am at four," he said, pointing to the 37-inch mark. "Here is Honey Moon at one. Here is Harvest at six months. But let's look at year eight — here I am. Here is Honey. And then what happens — at nine, and ten, and eleven, there is no more Harry. *Abracadabra.* Harry Moon has vanished from his own family's growth chart."

John Moon stood and looked intensely at Mary. He took a deep breath as he stared at the pencil marks on the wall. It was true. Harry's growth marks had simply stopped.

"But Harry Moon," said John, "that's just because you have been in a growth slump. It happens. Why tomorrow, you might wake up and have grown a foot. That's the way it works for some of us, son. Almost like magic."

"Or maybe you were ashamed of me. Admit it, Dad, you stopped measuring me because you were embarrassed to acknowledge that you had a runt for a son."

"We have never been embarrassed by you, son. Well, except for maybe that time at Tommy Patterson's seventh birthday when you messed your cargo pants..."

"I was allergic to red vines! Come on!" Harry said, throwing his head into his hands.

"I didn't mean that," John said. "I was just trying to lighten things up. We love you, Harry. And we could not be prouder."

Mary Moon said, "You are a good boy. We don't care how tall you are. You can't control that." She kissed his cheek. "But you can be strong. You can be smart. You can have a good heart. All the most important things that come from the inside. That is what makes you the loveable Harry Moon!"

"The loveable and SHORT Harry Moon. Just great." Harry folded his arms across his chest. He tried not to let his lower lip quiver but it was no use. Harry could not hold back the tear that worked its way down his cheek.

CLOCK PARTS

After his homework, Harry went to the garage. For over an hour he worked on his magic, trying to create a spell that would return his books to normal size. The print in his Grimoire was so tiny he had to use a powerful magnifying glass to read the recipes. After several failed attempts and making a bit of a mess, not to mention a cloud of disgusting odors, Harry came upon the antidote to bring his schoolbooks, his backpack and Grimoire back to regular size.

It was an exasperating experience, but Harry's dad had taught Harry to never, ever, *ever* give up. And Harry was not about to quit. Not when it came to getting his books back to normal size and certainly not when it came to growing bigger and older, as *fast* as he possibly could.

38

Harry sat on his wobbly stool at his garage worktable, a wormy old bench with gnarled knots and peeled paint. He thought and thought and then he thought some more until his mind landed on an entirely NEW idea.

"I think I am looking at this problem the wrong way. This is really about time. If Dad is right, I have to figure out how to speed up time. Yeah, that's it. If I could just figure out a way to get older faster, then I will grow and . . . and, well, at least I should grow *some*."

⟨⟩

For the next few days, whenever Titus Kligore found Harry in the school hallway and flicked the top of his head, Harry would become even more motivated.

"How's the magic coming, short stuff?" Titus would ask.

"It's coming," Harry always said.

It's coming alright, Harry thought. *But when?*

Over the next few days, boxes and cartons of different sizes arrived at the Moon front door. They were all addressed to Harry. He could always find things really cheap on the Internet. Besides, he wasn't old enough to drive so the computer was an easy way for a kid to get around. And he managed to save a few bucks from the magic shows he performed — mostly at birthday parties.

"What was all that commotion in the garage, Harry? Are we going to see a new magic trick?" his dad asked at the breakfast table.

Harry gulped down a bite of egg and cleared his throat. "I'm building a really fast clock to speed up time," he said.

"Oh, a science fair project? Hmmm, do you think it might speed up restoring my car? It's taking forever!" John asked. Harry's dad was restoring a 1995 MG-F that he bought in an auction in Greenville. The car was shiny and hunter green with a soft top and brown leather seats. "It is su-weet!" Harry's Dad would say with a happy lilt in his voice whenever he talked about it.

"This clock should speed up *everything*," Harry said. He gulped down his scrambled eggs. "I hope."

After school that day, Harry Moon got to work in the garage. He followed the instructions in the Grimoire down to the last detail, without the need of a magnifying glass now that he had been able to return the book to normal size.

He labored at his work bench in the corner of his dad's garage for days. When the final clock spring came in from Toledo, Ohio he carefully placed it into the space he had prepared inside the machine's inner workings. With a sigh, he stepped away from the bench. Harry thought he had finally done it.

Harry took a deep, deep breath as he admired his craftsmanship. The machine was a spectacular feat of engineering. Harry thought he was looking at the Taj Mahal of clocks. Harry's time machine was a thing of beauty.

The beautiful monster stretched a good two feet across the surface of the work bench. It was composed of thirteen different clock faces and fifteen separate clock works. On the floor in front of the gorgeous beast was an old kitchen chair with a red vinyl seat that Harry's mom said he could use for his endeavor.

41

The chair was secured with bungee cords to the clocks. According to the Grimoire, after winding the first clock, the other clocks would also start to rotate. As the user declared "Abracadabra," he or she would plunk down in the chair and time would speed up in the user's life.

Well, look at you, now," said Rabbit, appearing from a corner of the garage. "You are really something, aren't you, Harry Moon?" Rabbit scratched the scruff of his chin with his paw as he hop-walked closer to the young magician.

"I might be something great when this time machine gets through with me!"

"So you think it is a good idea to go against the natural order of things to get your way? Isn't good mischief about working *with* life's elements, not working against them?"

Harry still couldn't take his eyes off the time machine. "Whaddaya mean, Rabbit?"

"The ocean ebbs and flows, the moon rotates with the sun, night becomes day, water nourishes the vegetables. The sun makes the flowers grow. You know, the natural order of things?"

"Oh, I see what you mean," Harry said scratching his forehead with a screwdriver. "But Rabbit, I am not messing up time. I am just giving it a ... a little push forward."

Rabbit hopped onto the bench. "Maybe it is best to be your own person and not worry so much about what Titus Kligore thinks." Rabbit blinked at Harry. After all, you're already taller than me."

"Hey, my life is not run by Titus Kligore. In fact, he owes me. I saved his life on Halloween at Chillie Willies, remember? And I should be taller than you. You're just a rabbit."

"Just a rabbit? That hurts."

"Come on. You know what I mean."

"I remember everything, Harry. I am a Rabbit with memory. I don't forget."

"You're like an elephant, then," said Harry.

"Except I'm not an elephant. I'm Rabbit." Rabbit leaned his furry elbow against the time machine. "Don't you think you should just get out of the way and let time move at its own

rate? Why speed life up? There is so precious little of it."

"Well, I don't want to speed up through the whole thing," said Harry. "I'm just speeding it up for a while. There is a taller Harry Moon out there somewhere and I want to find him. Wanna watch?" Harry tightened a small screw on the first clock. "Now is as good a time as ever to get this time machine party started."

"I will watch for a while." Rabbit sighed.

45

Harry looked at his wrist watch. It was exactly eight o'clock. He ran over to the key that controlled the master spring on the time machine. Harry took a deep breath and steadied himself. With his right hand he turned the key as tight as he could without damaging the spring component. He ran over to the chair.

With a very loud and commanding, "ABRACADABRA," Harry plunked into the chair. Both hands clasped the bottom of the seat as he held on for dear life. His heart pounded so hard he thought he could hear it over the ticking of the clocks.

Harry Moon turned his head to watch the dials on the machine. One by one, the hands on the clock faces began to turn, moving faster and faster and faster as the master spring gained momentum.

Harry smiled widely, quite proud of himself. *This is a wonder.* He looked around the garage. There was the lawnmower, the snow blower and his father's refurbished MG-F, but Rabbit was gone.

"Wow," Harry said. "He didn't watch for long. But, wait a minute, maybe this is actually working! Maybe Rabbit had been watching for quite a while! Maybe time is flying by!"

Harry looked down at his watch. "Hmmm," he said. "It is now eight o'clock *and two minutes.*"

Harry waited and waited and waited for time

to arrive and sweep him into the future.

Poor Harry. Time did not come.

48

4'2"

THE RAVENS WIN

Harry looked at his watch. It was now ten o'clock. He had been sitting in the time machine chair for two hours and it was now his bedtime. With a sigh as big as Titus Kligore's ego, Harry slowly stood. He kicked his foot against the workbench. "Darn time machine!" he hollered. The contraption wiggled and shook from the vibration of Harry's kick. "I did everything exactly like the book said. You should have worked."

Harry turned off the lights and locked up the garage. He had been so focused on the Time Machine he didn't even know it had rained. Must have been a downpour, too. He slogged through the backyard to his back door. He took a moment to pull himself together and decided to quench his frustration with a snack. He slipped into the kitchen and quietly closed the door behind him. He sniffed the air.

"Mmmm."

He smelled something and he was pretty sure it was not one of Mom's apple pies. "That's it," he said snapping his finger. "Fresh paint. Wonder who's painting."

There in the threshold to the dining room was his mom. She had laid down newspaper on the floor and was painting over the penciled growth marks (and Harry's non-growth) on the wall.

"Mom, you didn't need to do that," Harry

said.

"I did, Harry," said Mary Moon. "You know why?"

"Why, mom?" Harry moved closer to his mother.

"Because your height is not important. What is important is that!" She pointed with her brush at the words on the wall. They had been stenciled across the room where the wall met the ceiling. They had been there for as long as Harry could remember. *Joy, Peace, Love, Patience, Kindness, Faithfulness, Gentleness, Goodness, and Self-Control.*

"Thanks, Mom. I know you are right, it just takes time to figure life out, you know?"

"Exactly," said Mary Moon. "It takes time. But always remember what we tell you."

"What's that, Mom?"

"Test those spirits." Mary Moon wiped her

fingertips on an old rag. "This is so important, Harry, especially with your magic and the spirit world. When you are looking for answers, we humans need to test everything.

Harry sat at the kitchen table. He fidgeted with the salt shaker. "You're right about that too," he said.

"You don't want to go running with the wrong crowd of spirits," Mary Moon said. "Who knows what was really going on with that big bike? Or who knows what is really going on with that Time Machine you are working so hard on out in the garage?" His mom dipped her brush in the small paint can. "There is a whole unseen world around us, Harry Moon. Much good, some not so good. We must love what is right and hold tight to the truth."

"Yeah, right again," he said. "It's just so hard sometimes."

"Who knows why you were designed in this unique way? But I love every part of you!" she said. "Maybe one day, you'll be the only one

who is compact enough to crawl through an air vent and save somebody's life."

"Compact. That's one way to describe me, I guess. Maybe, one day," Harry said. "I guess that will be something to look forward to. Goodnight, Mom."

He leaned down and kissed his mom on the head forgetting about the snack.

"I love you, Harry," she said.

"I love you, too, Mom."

Harry watched as his mom continued to paint. The white brush erased the number *four feet, two inches.* Vanished like magic.

If only life could be that easy. He walked up the steps to bed.

For a few days after the Time Machine debacle Harry felt a little better. He got back to his usual routine and even went to the high school football game with Declan

53

Dickinson, Hao Jones and Bailey Wheeler. They were cheering as the Sleepy Hollow Ravens trounced the Acton Mavericks, twenty-seven to nothing and it was just the second quarter.

And then, as if by magic, Sarah Sinclair was standing right next to them with a smile that only she possessed.

"Mind if I join you guys?" she asked looking directly at Harry.

"You bet!" Harry said, scooting over to make room. He felt his face flush when Declan nudged Bailey's ribs and snickered a little.

Sarah wiggled in right down next to Harry, shoulder to shoulder. There was no height difference now. They were equals, head-to-head, face-to-face. *And, wow. She looked great.* Sarah was wearing a navy blue peacoat and a red scarf. He could smell her favorite perfume that she must have dabbed behind her ears. It was the same perfume she had been wearing since she first babysat for him. *She still smells great.*

"How's the Junior play going?" Harry asked.

"It's daunting," she said. "Still learning all the lines and all the dances. We all have been working until eleven every night. I think this is the first time I have been outside in a month." Sarah gave Harry a smile, her eyes twinkling.

55

"It's the only way to do it," Harry said. "You have to be tenacious. Elia Kazan said it's that last five percent that makes all the difference and you have to leave it on the floor."

"Who's Elia Kazan?" Sarah asked.

"The stage and film director. *On the Waterfront? Streetcar Named Desire?*"

"You know so much," Sarah said, squeezing his arm.

"NOT a big deal. He likes old movies, that's all," said Declan.

"I know he really loves movies," Sarah told Declan. Harry's friend sat up straight. Being acknowledged by a high school junior was a huge deal. That doesn't happen every day.

"We had to call your Dad when you wanted to watch *Behold a Pale Horse* on cable," said Sarah, looking at Harry. "Do you remember?"

"Well, that's because they were classics and

not streaming," Harry said.

"Really? Classics is just another name for really, really old movies," muttered Declan. "BORING."

"Well, I love the classics, too," Sarah said. "I was always happy when your dad said ok."

Harry was having a great time with Sarah, just hanging out and catching up. That was until the Sleepy Hollow Ravens scored another touchdown. The fans all rose to cheer their team. Harry's heart broke a little. When he and Sarah stood with the crowd, he was once again, the short kid next to his one time babysitter who happened to be a good six inches taller.

"Sarah. Do you think I'll ever be as tall as you?"

"Are you kidding? I'm not tall. I'm actually a pipsqueak compared to the other girls in class." Sarah turned toward his face and looked deep into Harry's eyes. "Of course,

Harry Moon. One day. You will be just tall enough."

"I just wish it happened already," he said.

Sarah shook her head Her eyes crinkled. "Harry, isn't that part of the magic of life?"

"What?"

"Seeing how the story plays out? Like the classics we used to watch on TV? Like on the stage? Or on the football field here tonight, or in life?" Another loud cheer from the stands rang out. "We think we know but we don't. We can plan and we should, for sure, but there are things out of our control. Some things we just have to wait for."

"That's my problem, Sarah. I'm a magician so I should be able to do stuff that nobody else can do. I get confused, sometimes, when I have to wait."

As soon as he said the words Harry remembered what Samson Dupree had said.

It is best not to use magic when you are confused.

60

OINK

We trounced them," said Hao after the game. "Fifty six to three. Yikes. We are beasts. They should put us in a cage and feed us raw meat."

"Trounced?" Sarah said. "More like destroyed."

"It was a massacre," Harry said.

It took a while but the stadium emptied

out and Harry and his friends were standing outside waiting for their rides. Sarah and Bailey were getting picked up by their moms. Bailey's mom came first. She honked and Bailey dashed to the mini van. Harry stood alone with Sarah, chatting about small things, like the game and history tests until Sarah's mom arrived. Harry watched until Sarah was safely in her mom's car. "Come on, Hao," he said as he watched the car drive off. "We better get home too."

62 Harry walked Hao as far as his house and then turned onto Nightingale Road. As he walked home, he saw a dog on the other side of the road. The dog was sitting back on its haunches like it was waiting for him. Harry walked across the road and approached the mangy canine. It was Titus Kligore's butt-ugly, stinky dog, Oink.

Harry did not much like Oink. Titus's dog was a mutt with a lot of "pit bull" in him. Harry thought he was about as gross-looking as any dog could get. Oink slobbered a lot and smelled like the bottom of a garbage can.

"Where's your costume, Oink?" Harry asked.

"I just can't fool you, Harry," the beast said with a disgusting slobber and a lick of his chops. "Or can I?"

"Ehh, keep your spit mess away from me. Why don't you go home to your boss man, Titus," Harry said. Titus Kligore had been a bully to Harry for as long as he could remember. Titus even cut Harry's hair off with a pair of giant shears. But ever since Harry saved his life at the Halloween party, Titus had been acting almost normal to Harry. A little rough, to be sure, but almost, kinda nice. A tiny bit nice. Ok, maybe, just not so mean. Anyway, a definite improvement over Titus's hair-slashing days.

63

"Yeah, I can tell him you're still short."

"Go ahead. I don't care."

"Sure you, do Harry. You care. You care a lot."

"Well it was Titus who got me really thinking about this whole height thing to begin with," Harry said. "*Use your magic on yourself,* he says. Fat lot of good his advice did for me. I should NEVER EVER have listened to him."

"That's the problem," Oink said, brushing up and rubbing his leg up against Harry's pant leg.

"Hey, get out of here! Don't get so close and don't ever touch me!" Harry yelled out to the repulsive creature. "You are gross! I like it better when you wear costumes and don't play your butt-ugly self so I don't have to see so much of you at once!"

"You need an expert, buddy," Oink said, ignoring all of Harry's yelling. "Someone really smart to help you figure out your troubles." The malodorous mutt head-butted Harry's butt. "You shouldn't be relying on that silly Grimoire from Samson Dupree. You need to go smarter. You need professional magic from a pro."

"What do you know?" Harry said. "You are just an ugly pile of drool!"

"No, that's not quite true," said Oink as he walked with Harry down Maple Street. "I am also part wolf."

"Well, none of that matters. We both know that dogs and wolves can't talk!" said Harry. "Only demons from hell that look like butt-ugly dogs can talk."

"But your Rabbit talks, Mister Harry!" Oink said. His big, brown eyes looked up at Harry. He wagged his chopped off tail, pretending to be his friend. "You see, Harry, dogs were once wolves, but the wolf part was bred out of most dogs. But not me. I am special. You know what wolves do?"

65

"What? So what do dogs-that-think-they-are-wolves from hell do?" Harry asked, becoming quite annoyed. He was not too happy that his peaceful walk was interrupted by this particular smelly, pit-bull mutt. He took a whiff of his sleeve to make sure he was not picking up the animal's terrible odor. He would have much rather spent the time savoring how sweet it was to see Sarah at the game.

"We survive, Harry," snarled Oink, whose big, eyes narrowed into a scowl.

"So what? What EXACTLY is your point, Oink?"

"You need to survive, Harry. It's a big, bad, and very, very tall, world out there, pal. Buildings are taller now. People are taller. If you want to compete, you absolutely need to get bigger. Titus was very right."

Harry stopped walking. He felt something

churn in the pit of his stomach. How low could his life sink? He was now listening to Oink.

"I know people who know people, Harry," Oink continued, hiding his snarl inside a look of compassion. "They can help you. I wasn't born yesterday. Not by a long shot. I have spent my fair share of time roaming the earth."

"So," Harry said.

"Sooooo, I met a lot of people."

Oink growled as a skinny, black cat slinked past. "Sleepy Hollow is not my only hangout you know. I have been to Boston to meet with the big boys and girls at *Fire Magic: All in One*. I have told them of your little . . . er sorry. Let's just say . . . problem. They can fix you right up. You just have to go and see them. They are pros."

Harry swallowed. "Your connections don't impress me. I know who you are. You should be thrown in a cage with no way out."

"Really?" Oink said. "Really?" He ran ahead of Harry and then stopped and turned. He sat back on his haunches, growling. "Let's stop playing games. You know I'm a dog like Rabbit is a rabbit."

"You're the devil," Harry said.

Oink licked a gob of slobber from his saggy jowls. "Harry, Harry, that's so old school, buddy. There is no devil. I'm just a wolf-dog with some BIG ideas who happens to know people. After all, you saved my master Titus's life. The least I could do is show you a little love."

"I already have a rabbit. And last time I checked, wolves like to eat rabbits."

"Only when they're famished," said Oink. "But I would be happy if you made the introduction to this rabbit of yours. I'm sure we could become good friends. Maybe I could take him to dinner." He licked his chops again.

They stopped in front of Harry' house. "It

stops here, pal. Don't think you are coming in," said Harry as he crossed the intersection of Maple and Nightingale. Harry headed to the back door.

"I wouldn't dream of it, PAL," Oink shouted. "Besides I have told you all you need to know. My friends at Fire Magic, 999 Gehenna Street in Boston are waiting to help you with this size thing. Think BIG, Harry."

"Go on, Oink, get out of here!" said Harry. "Beat it. My house smells like cookies are in the oven. Don't want you smelling it up!"

The sidewalk was silent. Harry reached into his pocket for his house key. He looked over at where Oink had stood but the ugly mutt was gone.

70

WOLVES AND RABBITS

"Titus Kligore and Oink are both playing you, man," said Hao on Skype. He and Harry were Skype chatting on their computers. "This 'let's get you big" stuff is just a ginormous sham to get you where they want you.".

"And just where do they want me?" asked Harry.

"In Titus's Dad's evil empire, of course!" Hao Jones was big into conspiracies.

"Yeah, that ain't happening," Harry said.

"Careful, my friend. You know Chillie Willies is a front for evil. How do you think the guy became Mayor? Maximus Kligore gets what he wants because he made a deal with DARKNESS!"

12

Hao leaned back in his desk chair. "Why don't you see for yourself, genius? I betcha even that *Fire Magic: All In One* store is also part of Kligore's *We Drive By Night* machine! They want you, Harry, because you have magic powers that'll fit perfectly into their Sleepy Hollow toolkit of horrors!"

"Toolkit of horrors? Sheesh, where do you get all this stuff? I'm not afraid of any of them, especially the Kligores, father or son." Harry wiggled his hands in the air and made a funny face.

"Really? I am not the one arguing with dogs

named Oink, man. But I do believe in that crazy rabbit of yours, so I am going to take you at your word."

"Thanks," said Harry.

"Okay, okay. Just don't get sucked in, that's all." Hao's tone was more relaxed. "Turning a bike into something the size of an airplane is enough drama for the month."

Harry laughed as he signed out of Skype. However, he did not close his browser. He was curious about the address that Oink had given him. Harry typed 999 Gehenna Street, Boston and gave it a click.

Google took him directly to the storefront of the *Fire Magic: All In One* store. A large emerald dragon lifted its throat and roared into the sky from Harry's computer screen. As the dragon roared, silver sparklers jettisoned from its mouth, lighting up the sky around it. The dragon was part of the storefront which was two stories high.

Man, that is one cool home page!

Harry Moon clicked the *Fire Magic* products tab. He was surprised to see so many items. There were table tricks, simple illusions, black hats, mirrors and spells pre-packaged with "all the necessary ingredients". Harry leaned into the screen for a better look. He clicked again, even more mesmerized by the design and amount of product on the website.

But Harry felt someone staring at him. He knew who it was without even looking. His sister, Honey Moon, was as noisy as the fifth level of *Grand Theft Auto*, but Rabbit was not. When Rabbit showed up it was more like a feeling so he didn't even bother to turn around and check.

"Looks pretty great, huh?" said Rabbit.

"It sure does!" said Harry. "And the prices aren't bad either!"

75

"Of course." Rabbit sat on the edge of Harry's bed, lounging in a navy blue velvet robe with matching slippers. "That's how they start reeling you in. One thing leads to another, you know."

"What do you think?" asked Harry. "You don't think it's cool?"

"Probably not in the same way you do," replied Rabbit.

"But you're not going to stop me from

going?" Harry asked with a squeak in his voice.

"I can only guide you, encourage you, warn you. Your decisions, Harry, must be your own. That's how life works, remember? Your choice."

"Then I choose to take the Amtrak to Boston!" said a very happy Harry.

Rabbit scratched behind his left ear. "That's up to you."

Harry glanced at the site again. "I don't think I really need to totally fill in my parents on this," he said. "Do you?"

"Again, that's up to you, too," said Rabbit, with a little wiggle of his whiskers.

"They would worry about me being alone in the city, don't you think?" said Harry. "Why put them through that mess?"

"If that's what YOU think," said Rabbit.

Harry scrolled through the webpage for a

moment. He was just about to say something when he noticed that Rabbit was gone.

78

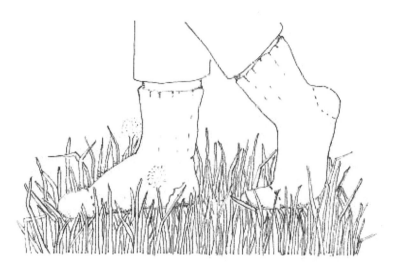

999 Gehenna Street

"Boy." Harry Moon yawned and stretched his arms up for effect at the dinner table. "It has been one tough week at school!"

"Science got you down, Harry?" John Moon asked.

"It's a lot of work."

"I thought so," his dad said as he plowed into the fresh-baked rhubarb pie slathered with whipped cream. "They are really pushing science these days."

"I wished they pushed more literature," said Mary Moon with a sigh.

"So, if it's alright," Harry said, in the midst of another exaggerated yawn, "can I be excused? I really need to get some sleep."

"Sure," Mary Moon said. "Don't forget to brush your teeth."

Honey Moon squinted at her brother suspiciously. "Mnmm. Leaving the dinner table early so you can go to bed. Who goes to bed early when it isn't even a school night?"

Harry wiped his mouth on his napkin and smiled brightly at his sister.

"A kid who is responsible like your brother," said Mary Moon with affection and pride. "Someone who is in control of his capacities

and knows when it is time to play and when it is time to rest. Isn't that so, Harry?"

"Yes, Mom," said Harry, with a smidgen of guilt in his voice. He stood and shoved his chair under the table which made Half Moon yelp.

"Nightie, night, Harry Moon," said Harvest from his high chair.

Harry walked over to his baby brother and tousled the fine, wispy hair on his head. "Bye-bye, Harvest Moon. I mean, nighty-night."

"Your brother, Honey is what we call a wholesome person," said John Moon.

"Wholesome?" said Honey Moon. She wrinkled her nose at the sound of the word.

"Oh no, Honey," said John. "Wholesome is not a bad thing. It's a very good thing."

"What is it?" asked Honey. "If that is what Harry is."

81

"It's when the whole person, every part — heart, mind, soul, and body — are working together for good purposes, for themselves and others."

"And THAT'S what you think Harry is?" asked Honey as she sized up her brother walking towards the stairway in the foyer. She shook her head.

John Moon swallowed a bite of pie. "That's right, Honey. Harry is a wholesome kid. When his body says he needs to rest, he doesn't think that he needs to run around on Friday night. He takes a reasonable, heartfelt approach and decides 'I must rest' so he can get the most out of his Saturday and Sunday."

As Harry marched up the stairs to his bedroom, Honey became no less suspicious. "IS THAT WHAT YOU ARE DOING, HARRY MOON?" she called out from the dining room. "Are you being wholesome? Are you really?"

"THAT'S EXACTLY WHAT I AM DOING," Harry shouted without turning around as he trudged up the stairs.

Before Harry even hit the second story landing, he knew he had already told four lies in less than sixty seconds. He said he was tired (he wasn't). He said science was hard (it wasn't). He was going to bed (anything but). He was wholesome (not anymore).

Harry hung the KEEP OUT sign on his doorknob and then slipped off his shoes and stepped out into the hallway, closing the door to his bedroom. He tiptoed down as quiet as he possibly could. Just like the rest of the town of Sleepy Hollow, his house was really old and had a tendency to creak. Harry had discovered if he walked very close to the walls, the floor boards stayed quiet. He scooted down the back stairway that led to the backyard and the garage.

While crickets sang and fireflies flitted in the early autumn night, Harry picked his way thru the darkness, careful not to alert the neighbor's dog. Harry snuck around the 1995 MG-F convertible that his father backed out of the garage so he could start his Saturday morning polish early.

Harry grabbed the house ladder that was leaning against the side of the garage and walked it across the driveway and lawn. Without making a sound, Harry lifted up the ladder and with a deft touch, Harry maneuvered the wooden steps up against the side of the house and propped it underneath his bedroom windowsill. Harry made sure that the ladder was secure in the ground before he left it there. As quietly as he had exited the house, Harry crept back inside. He slinked up the back stairway in

his stocking feet, now wet from the dew of the backyard grass.

When John Moon checked Harry's room later and found his bedroom door locked, he didn't think much of it. He had no reason not to believe his son was deep asleep.

Of course, Harry was being bad. What else could you call it? He had lied to everyone at the dining table (except for Harvest and Half Moon who was asleep under the table), and was sneaking out in the middle of the night to hop the local Amtrak that would speed carry him into Boston. Harry felt terrible about what he was doing but it still didn't keep him from doing it.

As Harry sat alone on his ride into Boston, a familiar friend walked down the aisle of the train and sat in the comfy seat next to him.

"Nice night for danger, Mr. Moon," said Rabbit as he looked through the train window at the dark, passing landscape.

"Hey, what are you doing here?" asked Harry. "You were the one who told me I have free choice."

"You do," said Rabbit. "That doesn't mean I have to like it."

"I don't know if I want you here. Sometimes I feel like you are a bit of an albatross around my neck," Harry said.

Rabbit looked at him and twitched his nose.

"Hey, I've read Herman Melville, too, you know," said Harry. "I'm no dummy if that's what you are thinking."

"I don't think you are a dummy. But *The Rime of The Ancient Mariner* wasn't written by Melville," said Rabbit. "It was Samuel Coleridge."

"Whatever. The point is how can I have any fun when you are poking at me like you do?"

"You call this fun, Harry?" asked Rabbit looking out the window. The Amtrak train was passing through Cambridge. They would soon be in Boston.

"Well, it's kinda fun. Maybe." Harry squirmed in his seat.

"Well, there, you have it. There's your fifth lie of the night. Is this REALLY your idea of having fun?"

"Who cares about lying if no one finds out?" said Harry. "I am doing this and no one will ever know."

"But I am on to you," said Rabbit. "And that's the way it has to be, Harry. You can never pull the ski cap over my eyes. I told you after we were introduced as nicely as I could, that having a friend like me is going to have consequences."

Harry looked out the window but all he could see was Rabbit's reflection. "Yeah," said Harry, very low, almost in a whisper. "You're right, Rabbit, you did say that."

"I only want the best for you, Harry."

"I believe you." Harry sighed.

"And I wish you didn't see me as a burden," said Rabbit. "I think I am more like a lark that sings a new song every morning when the sun breaks the horizon."

88

"How about if I just see you as my rabbit?" asked Harry.

"That'll do, too," answered Rabbit.

Harry walked down the aisle of the train. It was mostly empty, just a few people. Most commuters had already returned home from Boston for the weekend. Harry was just arriving in the city.

Harry knew Sleepy Hollow like the back of his hand. But this was Boston. It was huge and dark and . . . different. All he really knew was his destination — 999 Gehenna Street.

A Boy of His Word

A fog had blown in from the harbor, laying a thick mist on the streets giving an eerie glow to the street lights and making it difficult to see very far in front. But Harry had his cell phone and thanks to Google Maps, Harry knew *Fire Magic: All In*

One store was only a half-mile away from the train station. Even in the thick fog Harry was able to watch the small blue spot that represented him on the screen. Harry felt pretty proud of himself.

He walked three blocks on Chestnut Street until he turned left onto Paul Revere Avenue. He walked one block and then made a right onto Gehenna Street. From there, it was simply a fast pace of three blocks until he hit his destination. *A very fast pace.*

Hmmmm, he thought examining the screen on his phone. He turned the Google map upside down as if it were a snow globe, and saw 999 Gehenna become 666. "That's pretty weird," he said out loud. He started coughing as if something had gotten stuck in his throat. *Just a coincidence.*

"Or was it?" he heard Rabbit say in his mind.

"Rabbit, are you there?"

"Am I?" the voice of Rabbit seemed to say.

"Just because I am hidden from view, does that mean I am not here?"

Harry shook the voices from his head as fast as he unlocked the phone. The Google map returned to 999 Gehenna Street. He looked at the 7/11 Store with the address number 873. He was getting close. As he crossed the intersection of Gehenna and Edgar Allan Poe Blvd, he noticed the sidewalk ahead. The fog had lifted and the pavement was emerald colored.

91

Harry was amazed and intrigued by the color. He walked a few more yards and saw the emerald dragon storefront. The dragon pulsed green like a heartbeat. Its light bathed the buildings in every direction. It was just as it was on the website. But it was even more spectacular in person. Harry swallowed. Hard.

Harry had gone the distance. He was not looking at *Fire Magic* from a screen on his desk. He had lied, taken a train, walked a half-mile late at night and had finally arrived at the largest magic store in all of New

England — *Fire Magic: All in One* located at 999 Gehenna or (666 Gehenna depending on your point of view).

Harry stopped a moment on the green-colored sidewalk to admire the magnificent store in front of him. The Dragon's neck was erect, jutting up to the sky. Its terrible, green head reached into the night. From its open jaw, silver sparks flew into the dark, lighting the misty evening with silvery enchantments.

Fire Magic: All In One dazzled him. How could it not?

As Harry walked toward *Fire Magic*, he saw that the store didn't have a door. *That's not good for business*, he thought. The closer he got the faster Harry's mind whirled with ideas.

Harry had come to the massive talons of the dragon, reaching out as if to claw his skin off his body. In front of him was the bright, emerald belly of the beast. Harry shook his head in amazement. "Pretty cool." He reached out and touched the scaly skin of the dragon

that was the front wall of the store. "Ouch!" he yelped. The scales were sharp, like the spines of cacti.

"Open!" he said to the belly with confidence. But nothing happened. "Hello in there?" Harry leaned forward and knocked softly. "Hello? Anybody home?" He looked for a buzzer or laser sensor, *anything* that would allow a customer entry.

"Only special ones may enter," said a voice in Harry's head.

93

"Oink? Is that you?"

The voice of the smelly dog reverberated in Harry's mind. "Harry, you know it's me, buddy. Just because I am hidden, doesn't mean I didn't come along for the ride."

"What are you doing here?" Harry asked. "I told you to stay out of my house. How did you know I was coming?"

"I did stay out of Nightingale," Oink rasped

with a snarl. "But I traveled with you to make sure you knew just how special you really are."

Harry looked again for a buzzer or knocker.

"It is quite easy for you to enter," Oink said.

"Ah, I know," Harry said.

"Then if you know, just say it. It works for anyone when you acknowledge the spirit world."

94

"Don't I have to test the spirits?" asked Harry.

"Why?" said the voice of Oink. "In the end, we are all the same, buddy. Spirits are spirits."

Lost in the majesty of the reality before him, the great talons, the sky sparkling with dragon breath and the lustrous scales, Harry knew what he needed to do.

"Abracadabra," Harry commanded the scaly belly of the dragon.

Snap! Swirl! Snap! Swirl! Just like that, the belly dissolved into the night mist. Its scales grew dark as tar. In the gloaming, Harry saw the cavernous entry. He took one step and then another.

As he walked into the store, his nose was immediately hit with a foul smell, like an odor of cheddar cheese left on the counter for too long. The stench lasted only for a breath or two, but Harry thought it was as nasty as the smell on Oink running down the street while chasing a car. Harry passed through a curtain of red and white beads which hit his eyes and forehead as he walked through them.

The store was wallpapered in red velvet and tacked with buttons like you find on pricey living room sofas or your great grandmother's expensive winter coat. The place was loaded with great tricks. Harry saw them hanging on the walls or kept under glass. His heart raced with excitement.

Customers were everywhere, old men mostly

looking over the merchandise in silence. The cashier at the counter smiled at Harry Moon.

"Welcome, welcome." The young woman's face pulsed from a red strobe light that hung from the ceiling behind her. She was wearing a pair of cat ears and way too much makeup. "I'm BooBoo Hoodoo. I can tell you have come for the voodoo."

Harry Moon walked right up to the counter with so much confidence he swaggered. He liked this counter much better than the one at Sleepy Hollow Magic Shop. The *Fire Magic* counter was very low, made of black marble with reddish veins pulsing through it. Probably from the strobe. But still, it was pretty cool. Harry could look right at BooBoo Hoodoo without having to climb on an apple box or a barstool.

"I don't know about voodoo, Miss Hoodoo, but I would like to get some real magic."

She looked at Harry and smiled. She had the most dazzling smile, made all the more

white and sparkling in contrast to her bright, fire-engine-red lips. Harry had never seen teeth so white or wrapped inside of a more spectacular smile.

"Tired of the same old thing?" As Miss Hoodoo asked, she reached back toward the shelf behind her. There was a full stack of yellow *Doctor Magneto Amazing Magic for Eight to Twelve Years* boxes. Harry was impressed. He remembered how excited he felt when he opened the one he got for Christmas five years ago. It was his first magic set.

97

BooBoo Hoodoo looked again at the stack and then back to Harry. He could feel her power.

Yeah, Harry thought, *she is dressed kinda goofy and the red satin cat ears are a bit cornball, but she sure is pretty.* Her rosy-red cheeks were full and round. They looked like you could put them in a bowl and chomp them down like ice cream.

"I said, tired of the same old thing?" BooBoo Hoodoo asked for the second time.

"Oh, you bet."

"Well then, before we get started I have to tell you that I can not sell you fireworks." BooBoo Hoodoo leaned forward on the counter, looking into Harry's wide eyes. "In the state of Massachusetts, you must be eighteen years of age."

Harry bent his arm on the counter. He had never seen a woman so beautiful, except of course for his mom (and that was a different way) and his supercrush, Sarah Sinclair (but she did not see him as a proper boyfriend). *BooBoo Hoodoo is sooooooo beautiful,* he thought. He was in dreamland (or nightmare land depending on your perspective).

Harry had to swallow three times before he could speak. "I didn't come for fireworks, Miss Hoodoo," Harry finally said. "I came for magic. Like I told you."

"How much moola are you carrying? Are you carrying plastic? We take American Express, Visa and MasterCard."

"Two dollars and twenty cents," he said. "For the right magic, I will give you all I have."

He reached into his left pocket and pulled out two one-dollar bills and the twenty pennies. He slid the cash onto the counter but not so close for Miss Hoodoo to think it was hers . . . yet.

In the red light of the store, she leaned in, her face caught in the flames of the pulsing crimson light. "I thought you said magic. You only want a trick?" she asked.

"You were right the first time, Miss Hoodoo." Harry pulled himself up to his full height. "I am already skilled at the tricks of illusion as you probably can tell just by looking me over with your spirited eyes."

"Uhm, I see," BooBoo Hoodoo said with a purr. "You are quite the magician already."

99

"And I am all ready to put away childish things," Harry said. "I am looking for something far more incredible. I am looking for magic which will let me control time!"

BooBoo Hoodoo leaned forward. She brought her big smile and red lips closer to Harry.

"So are you *really ready* for that kind of magic?"

"I am soooooo ready, Miss Hoodoo."

"You do know that it's...er... dark magic?"

Her great cat eyes opened wide. She gazed at Harry with an understanding that he found utterly outstanding and so very charming.

"Dark magic, white . . . red, green or blue . . . what does it matter? Doesn't it all come from God?" Harry said.

She looked at him confused. She was a bit thrown as she gazed out at the red velvet waste land and the quiet men in their trench

coats and hats riffling through boxes of table tricks, Roman candles, and cherry bombs.

"I suppose you could say that's true, technically. But this shop, *Fire Magic: All In One* is a fully owned subsidiary of the *We Drive By Night Corporation*, doing business as an S Corp In the USA."

"Whatever. Still the Great Magician owns the whole kittenkaboodle, does he not? Now, show me what you got."

101

"Well, Mister . . . er . . . ?"

"Moon. Mister Harry Cornelius Moon." Harry pulled himself up to his full height . "And proud of it."

"Well, Mister Moon, are you prepared to spend the full two dollars and twenty cents or are you just teasing me?

"I am a boy of my word."

"Then, for that kind of money, Mister Moon,

I am going to ask my special assistant, Miss Cotton Candy, to join me for she knows the magic of time."

"Join away, Miss Hoodoo."

For the first time, Harry realized the cashier with the satin cat ears was wearing a leopard print jumpsuit. Miss Hoo-doo of the *We Drive By Night S Corp* (with the "S' having nothing to do with Federal regulations and everything to do with that certain word, Snake), clapped her hands. "Abracadabra!" she commanded.

The pink air behind Miss Hoodoo began to spin, taking on the form of a mini tornado. It spun and spun and then . . . out of the cone of the storm rose the most remarkable assistant of magic that any magician could ever dream of having. This was Cotton Candy dressed in a crocodile leather dress. Her hair was pink and wild as the wind that just produced her. Cotton Candy's eyes were dark and set within a heart-shaped face.

103

"I'll take it!" Harry cried.

"You would need a kingdom of gold to purchase her," said Miss Hoodoo with a smile.

Harry laughed, seized by the magic moment of Cotton Candy's dazzling arrival.

104

THE HARRIEST NIGHT

From the other side of the counter, Harry watched Miss Candy show off her powers. He watched her place a seed in a red, plastic cup on top of the counter. Within seconds, a giant beanstalk rose from the cup. Its vine crashed through the roof of the *Magic Fire: All In One,* shooting into the sky, climbing into the dark night.

"Wow, what was that?" Harry said. "How did you do it?"

"That is what time looks like, under our control, Mister Moon," said Cotton Candy.

The beanstalk was bigger and taller than the old oak tree in the center of Sleepy Hollow Square near the statue of the Headless Horseman.

Like an expert swordsman, Cotton Candy took her hand and swiped it through the trunk of the beanstalk. Just like that, without Miss Candy even saying Abracadabra, the beanstalk vanished. The red cup was the only thing that remained.

"Was that an illusion?" asked Harry, his eyes wide. "You did not give me a chance to analyze it properly."

Cotton Candy leaned across the counter. Her lips were as pink as Miss Hoodoo's were red. She stared at Harry.

"That, Mister Moon, was not illusion. That was magic."

As Harry looked at her, the temperature of his blood rose. His brow broke into a sweat. Cotton Candy's eyes were brown but they grew black as Harry stared into them. He couldn't turn away. He was falling into a trance. As his mind sank into the black pitch of her eyes, Harry discovered that it was dark all around him.

Harry looked deep into the darkness. A young woman emerged. She walked as if she was in a dream. She wore a silver ball gown and golden slippers. She looked familiar to him. But why? Who was she?

"Is that . . . Cinderella?" asked Harry in a whisper.

"Of course not," laughed Cotton Candy. "That is Sarah Sinclair."

Harry looked at the attractive, young woman.

"Oh yeah," he said carefully watching. He could see the freckles on her nose, those

107

unmistakable dimples in her cheeks when she smiled. Harry pegged her as being about twenty-five years old. "Wow! She turned out beautiful," Harry said.

"I would call that *gorgeous* myself, but you are the poet, Mister Moon," replied Cotton Candy.

"Where are we?" he asked. A handsome prince marched out of the darkness and took Sarah's hand.

"We, Mister Moon, are in 'a time yet to be'. Heard of that phrase?

"What does it mean?

"That line, 'a time yet to be.' Surely you recognize it from the sacred writings."

With her silver gown flowing around her, Sarah Sinclair danced with the handsome prince. She was leggy and tall but the prince was even taller.

"Is that who I think it is?" Harry said, staring into the dark limbo of the trance. Sarah turned, and Harry could see it was Titus Kligore, all grown up.

"Why wouldn't it be him, Harry?" Cotton Candy said. "He comes from the wealthiest family in Sleepy Hollow. No doubt, some day, he will follow in his father's footsteps and become the mayor. That is, unless you allow me to control your time." But all Harry could hear was her voice. He was alone in the dark with the dancing couple who looked like they had jumped off the pages of a fairytale book.

"How are you controlling time?" asked Harry looking into the darkness for Cotton Candy.

"With my very breath," Miss Candy replied.

As she spoke, the wind blew in the darkscape of Harry's vision. When Sarah turned again in the slow dance, Titus Kligore had vanished. Sarah's dancing partner was now a different prince.

It was Harry Moon as a man. It was undeniably him! There was his black hair falling over his head as if an ink bottle had exploded on it. There were his bright eyes. He was smiling. He was a pretty good dancer and he was really, *really* enjoying himself. But best of all, he was tall enough, as Sarah had said, a good three inches taller than Princess Sarah.

"You can do that with the future with your breath?" whispered Harry.

"That's real magic, kiddo," smiled BooBoo Hoodoo with the voodoo. "It's even better than your lagomorpha magic."

"Lagomorpha?" Harry.

"Yes, better than rabbit magic. And for the two dollars and twenty two cents that you have placed on the counter, that future could be yours," said Cotton Candy.

"Miss Candy," said Harry Moon, "you have yourself a deal!"

When he said the word, 'deal', it was as if Harry had said 'Abracadabra'. The dark vision vanished. Princess Sarah and Prince Harry had vanished, also. Harry was back in

111

the lobby of the *Fire Magic: All in One* store.

Across the black, marble counter were the two salespeople, BooBoo Hoodoo and Cotton Candy, looking as colorful as two peaches on an August day.

"We have quite a company here," said BooBoo. "Our boss takes the magic of controlling time very seriously."

"That's what I want, Miss Hoodoo! I want time magic."

"Well, you have come to the right place, Mister Moon," said Cotton Candy. "I can give you the breath that will get you taller, wiser and dancing with Sarah in no time."

"Is it that obvious? I mean about my height?" Harry asked, shyly.

"You're a dwarf," Cotton Candy replied.

"Well, I have been assured that I will be having a growth spurt but not for several years. I do trust Mister Samson Dupree . . . ."

"Samson Dupree?" Miss Hoodoo screamed in laughing disdain. "That tired old thing? Is he still around?"

When Cotton heard the name, she started shrieking as well. The laughter filled the store.

"You know him? He owns the Sleepy Hollow Magic Shop."

"Child, he doesn't own anything! At best, he's renting! He is lying to you. Don't listen to him. Sleepy Hollow? That dumpy sinkhole? He might as well be selling out of Detroit! Mark my word, Detroit will be going down and so will that trash town of Sleepy Hollow. We had worked that out with Benedict Arnold long ago but he was hung before the corporation could conclude the deal with England!"

113

"Wait a minute, Sleepy Hollow is my little town. It may be small and we have a few problems here and there but it is my town!"

"We'll just see what happens to that little town of yours once our master plan takes hold. I hear it's Halloween every night out there." Miss Hoodoo and Cotton Candy laughed again so hard that they both snorted.

"I don't know what you are talking about and I don't really care. For now, I just want to focus on *what I want*. And I want to buy the time magic! If I can buy time, then I can be smarter. Better. Taller. Just like you said."

"Very well," said Miss Hoodoo. "If that's all you want *for now*. Cotton and I were just thinking that a talented fellow like you could be an important player in the long term growth of our...Corporation."

"I am not looking for a job. I already have one. It's called eighth grade!" Harry said. He was disturbed by the laughter about his friend, Samson Dupree. These women could not possibly understand what made Samson special.

"Just give me the time!" he said. He was so wound up, he was practically shouting.

"We will need the full two dollars and

twenty cents," Miss Hoodoo demanded. Her voice went from soft to flinty, almost sharp.

"Yes, that's what I said. I am a boy of my word!" replied Harry. He pushed the money over to their side of the counter that now seemed to pulse red even stronger.

Miss Hoodoo counted the money one last time. She smiled, affirming the money was all there. She hit the cash register and distributed the bills and change into the tray.

115

Miss Candy and Miss Hoodoo went to the back shelf and opened a golden cabinet, removing a red paper bag. Harry watched as Miss Hoodoo opened the sack. Miss Candy stretched her neck upward as if she were a wolf getting ready to howl at the moon. She inhaled all the air that she could. Then Miss Candy turned to Miss Hoodoo and nodded.

Miss Hoodoo picked up a wand made from peppermill wood that was at the edge of the counter. She waved the poisonous wand over Miss Candy's head. "Abracadabra," Miss

Hoodoo said.

Miss Candy stood there, silent, holding her breath inside of her bursting lungs, her eyes bulging out of her face. When the air was ready, she leaned into the bag. She exhaled, hurling her breath into the red, paper sack. The bag inflated—filled with the magic breath of time.

With the hands of a surgeon, Miss Hoodoo snapped the bag closed and folded it three times. Then Miss Candy leaned in again and touched her lips to the last fold with her cotton candy-colored mouth, whispering words too low for Harry to hear.

"When you get home," Miss Hoodoo instructed, "sit on the edge of the bed. Before you open the bag, think of the Harry you truly want to be: Smarter. Taller. Better."

"Okay," Harry said, listening attentively.

"Then open the bag and breathe in what I have placed inside for you," coo-cooed Miss Candy. She had a warble as sweet as a turtledove.

"Okay. It's not like a pizza, is it?" Harry asked. "When it gets cold, is it different? I mean it will take me sixty minutes to get home. The hot air might be cold by then."

"Don't you think we know stuff like that?" BooBoo Hoodoo said with such exasperation that Harry knew his question did not require an answer.

117

"This will work. Look at me," Cotton said with an encouraging tone. She held her hands out at her side and turned slowly for Harry to see. "I am three-thousand and ninety-seven years old."

"That's ridiculous." Harry took another look. "Anyway, I don't want to get that old. Just make me a high school senior."

"Then sleep tonight as long as you can."

"Tomorrow is Saturday so that is easy," replied Harry.

"When you awaken, you will be as you envision yourself. You will be every bit the prince that you saw in your dream."

"Well, that Cinderella thing was more your thing than mine. But, if I can be taller than Sarah and Titus, then Saturday will be the most awesome day of my life!"

"You have what you want, now GO," said Miss Hoodoo.

"Fantastic! Thanks so much!"

Harry carefully picked up the red bag filled with air. He turned toward the hallway from where he came and then turned back. "Sorry about my little outburst, there," he said. "I just don't like it when people make fun of my town or my friends like Samson Dupree."

Miss Hoodoo and Miss Candy nodded, barely able to control the peeling laughter that stirred within.

"Go, go now," said Miss Hoodoo.

Harry hurried toward the dragon-maw door. His hairiest night had just begun.

120

LEAVING GEHENNA

Harry passed the ashen men in the store. It was odd, they seemed to not have moved an inch from their places in all the time that Harry had been at the *Fire Magic: All in One Store*. They seemed to be looking at the same box of tricks again and again and again.

"Good luck!" Miss Cotton Candy called out, in her coo-coo voice, buoyed with cheer.

"Good luck?" Harry thought as he made his way from the store. "There's no such thing as luck."

He walked down the aisle with his bag of time, once again, finding no door. But as he spoke, "Abracadabra," the portal revealed itself. He exited through the dark cavern just as he had entered it.

∞

"He'll be back," laughed Miss Hoodoo.

"Of course he'll be back. Once they come through that door, they always come back!" Miss Cotton Candy replied. Her cat eyes were just as dark as the dark magic held by Miss BooBoo Hoodoo.

"The *We Drive By Night* Corporation can use a kid like that," said Cotton with a hint of the sage in her voice.

◆

Harry Moon raced down dark Gehenna Street, retracing his journey back to the Boston Train Station. He was careful with his steps. He did not want to spill any time magic from the red paper bag The sack was light, of course, because it contained Miss Candy's hot air. Harry believed it needed expert handling. He carried the bag out in front with one hand, not two. Two hands felt clumsy. One hand gave him better balance.

He thought, *I must already be maturing. When I was a kid I would have been so nervous. I would have had to use both hands. Now, I know I can do it with one.*

He held the bag in front of him so he could get a good look at it. He was in a rough neighborhood in Boston, with a lot of run-down, vacant stores. Any number of thieves in the night, drunks, or standard muggers might attempt to steal the precious bag. What he didn't know is that there was absolutely no chance of that. The way he was handling it with his single arm outstretched, the people in the neighborhood thought he was carrying a bag of dog poo.

There was a ten o'clock train back to Sleepy Hollow. Harry breathed a sigh of relief when he arrived at the station to see by the wall clock that he had five minutes to spare. The train ride back to Sleepy Hollow was only twenty-seven minutes, but as Harry settled into his seat, he knew it would seem like an eternity.

124

He held the bag in a tight grip on his lap, keeping both eyes locked on it as he rode the train. He noticed the pink lipstick smear from Miss Candy's mouth on the red fold.

Harry Moon thought about Cotton Candy as the train made its way back to Sleepy Hollow. Maybe they were right about Samson. *With his crown and slippers and his store that never had any customers, Samson Dupree WAS a pretty unusual human being. But, then again, perhaps that was because Samson was not human at all.*

Twenty-seven minutes later and exactly on time, Harry walked home from the station, making sure to stay in the shadows of the maple, elm and oak trees that lined the streets. The sidewalks were bright with the light of the full moon. Harry crept along, quietly, not wanting to be spotted by his neighbors. They would absolutely spill the beans to his Mom or Dad if they saw him out late and unsupervised.

It was one of those hairy nights where you could hear every noise. He heard the night creatures crawling in the woods and the squirrels scrambling in the branches. It was so late that only two cars crossed Harry's path on the way home. One of them was black and had a promotional license for the *We Drive By Night* Corporation.

Harry remembered what his father had said once when he was cleaning the gutters. He had grabbed his back and said, "Growing old is no fun." Now, his son was mumbling the same words, only a little different.

Harry stood near the ladder that reached

to his bedroom window. He took a deep breath and whispered, "Being young is no fun either." It appeared to be difficult all around for the Moon men. But soon, he would be older, a tall teenager, and maybe even a senior at Sleepy Hollow High!

Harry had to hold the red bag in his mouth like a dog with a chew-toy. He figured it was safer to do that than to climb the old ladder with just one free hand. Slowly he went, rung-by-rung until he reached his window. With the skill of a cat-burglar Harry pushed the window open and slipped inside. Success!

Harry Moon had made it to Boston and back with no one knowing. He placed the bag on his bed in preparation for the magic ritual. He then went to the window and pushed the ladder away from the sill, watching it fall slowly into the yard because he knew his father would be up early to work on his convertible. CRASH! Harry winced. The ladder's clatter as it hit the lawn was a tad loud. Harry breathed a sigh of relief when he heard no stirring in the house from the crash.

The *All in One* witches had told Harry to sleep as long as he could after he breathed in the bag. He figured he would need to sleep until past noon. This was real magic after all. Not table illusion. Not Elvis Gold puffery. So Harry Moon, the hibernating bear, steeled himself ready for a long winter's nap in the middle of autumn on Nightingale Lane.

Harry slipped out of his jeans and into a pair of pajama bottoms. He flicked off the light. With reverence, he sat down on the bed in the bright moonlight. He picked up the bag and placed it on his lap.

127

There is no such thing as luck, he thought. *What were those women thinking?* He looked at the bag and thought about what his mother had said about testing the spirits.

There is only deep magic and dark magic, Harry thought. *How does anyone ever know for sure?*

Harry got on his knees at his bedside. He clasped his hands on his twin-sized mattress.

Harry Moon prayed, "Make it so. Make me a taller and wiser boy."

Harry climbed into bed, opened the bag and held it to his face. He breathed in as long as he could, trying not to gag. It was hard because it smelled as foul as the *Fire Magic* store, smelly cheddar left on the counter for too long.

Harry Moon closed his eyes and waited for the hot exaltation of Candy Cotton's spell to work.

Wiser. Bigger. Better. Taller.

He kept praying. He couldn't wait until the morning. He would have such long legs that he would no longer need Samson's barstool or an apple crate.

Harry Moon never had a hard time falling asleep. Except he did have trouble one Christmas Eve when his Dad had promised him an all expense paid trip to the Christmas Spectacular at Radio City Musical Hall.

But tonight, Harry Moon tossed and turned. He thought he was sleeping. He wasn't. He looked at his pillowcase. It was all wet from his sweat! He threw the pillow on the floor. Then for just a second, horror of horrors, Harry thought he had wet the bed. No, it was just his sweat and he was swimming in it.

He watched his alarm clock flip to 3am and sat up. His sheets were gone—top and bottom. Harry had tossed and turned so much he managed to completely strip his bed. All the sheets were on the floor. He thought he had already been through the hairiest and scariest part of the night. But maybe not. Maybe it was just beginning. He was in a panic. His heart pounded. His stomach churned. *What was happening?*

"You were supposed to be my friend," said a voice.

Harry grabbed onto the sides of his mattress. The bed was moving. His bed had turned into a raft. He was floating on a river. Dense, gray fog hung over the water. Then, sitting next to him Harry felt a familiar presence.

"Rabbit, is that you?"

"Of course it's me," said Rabbit.

Rabbit dipped a golden oar into the water, first one side then the other. He steered the raft down the wide river. "It would have been wonderful to grow up slowly with you, Harry. But no, not you, you had to go messing with time."

Harry looked around, trying to find something familiar but the river stretched on with no end, no land in sight. But, in the distance Harry saw the moon, bright and round. Harry squinted and shook his head. He even closed his eyes and opened them but there was no mistaking it. There was a man climbing up a long, long, wooden ladder. *He's trying to reach the moon.*

Rabbit navigated toward the moon. Although the water had turned choppy, Rabbit kept the vessel steady and true.

"Where are we?" asked Harry.

"We are riding the old river."

Harry reached into the water and swished his hand around. He was surprised how warm it was. He scooped some water into his palm. He smelled it.

"If this is a river, why is it hot, why is it . . . salty like the ocean?"

"Because it is your sweat and tears. Two very salty things my friend."

"Then why are you here?"

"You know the answer to that question. You and me have a thing going. I always got your back. Even when it's floating down river."

"Yes... I know but—"

132 "Well, how do you think you get wise? You get wise from me."

"So my prayer is being answered? Will I get taller? Wiser? Better?"

Rabbit continued to row, moving the oar with deft paws. "The truth, Harry Moon, is that all prayers are answered. Just not always the way you want or in accordance with your plans."

"What about answering the part of me getting taller? Will that happen?"

"Yes. In time, you will. Your time."

Harry took a deep breath as the pounding of his heart slowed to an gentle rhythm. The river turned smooth like they were floating on a river of silk. "I thought this dream was turning into a nightmare with all that sweat and tears stuff."

Rabbit pulled the oar from the water for a moment and looked at Harry. Rabbit raised an eyebrow in a wry arch, catching Harry's eye and when he did, they both laughed.

"It's really pretty simple, Harry. . . .

In the outside world and inside this one, look for the good in one another. We just have to do what's right. Doesn't make a bit of difference if you are, tall or small, wiser than Solomon, or better than everyone else. What's important is knowing that we belong to one another."

"Rabbit, where are we headed?" Harry asked.

"The same place we are always going. All our lives, Harry, all of us. We are all just

133

headed home."

Harry looked out at the river and to the moon still far in the distance. He saw the man again trying to climb the ladder. He looked closer and gasped. *Is that my father?*

The man kept climbing and climbing but never reached any higher.

"Is that my dad on that ladder?"

134

"Yes, it is, Harry."

"But why doesn't he get anywhere?"

"The rungs are broken. You have to fix that."

"Me? But how? What can I do?" Harry's heart pounded again.
"Those rungs are not just made from wood. They are made with trust. Trust between you and him. And you broke them."

"Oh. I see now." Harry sighed. "I never lied to him before. And tonight I sure told a doozy."

Rabbit continued to row. "You have to make that right."

Harry felt more warm tears slip down his cheeks. He tried to swipe them away, swipe them into the river.

"Come over here."

Rabbit held out his paw. Harry took it and was pulled upward, above his bed, above the river of sweat and tears.

Harry opened his arms first and Rabbit hugged him. The raft remained steady and true.

"It sure is beautiful," Harry said.

"What is beautiful?" asked Rabbit.

"That moon." Harry pulled away from Rabbit.

"That is you, Harry. That moon is you. Do you understand? You may be a little short for now. But you are still beautiful. Do you understand, my friend?"

Rabbit's right, Harry thought. *It doesn't matter how tall I am. I'm not really all that short and one day I will get taller. And even though I never would have chosen my Harry Moon name, it is still my name and I will make the best of it.*

As for searching for the deep magic, he supposed that Rabbit was right about that too. The real magic begins right here, right now, with all people. We must find the beauty in one another and hold on to that.

"Is this why you are here, Rabbit?"

"When you knock on a door looking for an answer, Harry, someone has to open it. Life will be a mystery to you for a very long time yet."

"Life *is* a mystery," said Harry Moon. "You know what they say, we humans may know a lot, but we understand little."

"Just keep knocking and learning," said Rabbit as he rowed on the river of anguish.

"Row with me, Harry, and I will never leave you."

Harry looked out at the moon. He saw the broken rungs clearly now and knew what he had to do. When Harry Moon glanced back to say something to Rabbit, he was gone, but not really. Harry knew he was there, just not seen. He was always there.

137

What started out to be the hairiest night was now an adventure. Harry Moon was on the river that flowed inside himself. He was going home to the moon, where the river was taking him. He had learned many things. And once again, he learned that Rabbit was always with him, even if he had messed up a bit.

"Now the real adventure begins," whispered Rabbit's voice.

"And I know why," Harry said as the raft

still floated down the river.

"Why?"

"My magic is not Sleight of Hand magic. I have the real magic."

"That's the ticket, Harry."

SATURDAY MORNING

The weekend had officially begun. It was six o'clock on Saturday morning. The larks were singing. First light was up and all seemed calm. The sun shone through Harry's bedroom window. There was the occasional sound of a car headed down street, the whirl of the paper boy's bicycle.

But the noise that happened next was like fingernails on a blackboard, or a cat's yowl piercing the quiet of the night. It started like a blender on low puree until it grew as loud as the blender on ice-crush.

It was highly unusual for John Moon to shout. At some point along the way it was somehow decided that there would be only one shouter in the family and that was Mary Moon, and generally only when she was calling out against the indignities of suburban life. But it was hard for Harry to hear his father screaming. The sound was screechingly sharp like ice cracking against the steel blade of that ice breaker.

Harry sat up in his bed with a feeling of dread. In his mind, he put together what probably had happened. It was all related to his sneaky adventure the night before and the deception he had created in order to have it.

As soon as he heard his father shout, "Emma, oh my Emma," he knew why the ladder he threw from the window made a noise that

was just a tad too loud.

"I'll get the hoodlums who did this!" John Moon said. "Just let me at 'em! Oh Emma. My sweet Emma!"

As he looked down at his legs, Harry also knew that he hadn't grown to be six-feet tall in the night. His pajama bottoms still fit fine.

With a heavy and guilty heart, Harry walked out of his room, down the stairwell at the rear of the house and through the back door. As the sun rose in the horizon, he headed across the dewy grass to the garage. Harry winced when he saw it.

There was the top of his escape-and-return wooden ladder broken, lying in pieces inside the guts of his father's green convertible MG-F. Emma was named after Emma Moon, his favorite great aunt who always wore green.

Harry winced again when he saw that the nails from the broken ladder had torn open the leather seats of the two seater and

141

broken the windshield.

John Moon had been especially proud that in the restoration of his auction-won car that he wasn't going to have to replace the tan upholstery. John had said proudly, "That leather is 100% original."

In fact on Friday night, he had just put a full

coat of saddle soap on the seats.

"We live in a good neighborhood, what kind of vandal would do this?" said John Moon as he looked to his son. Harry had never seen his dad cry before.

Harry swallowed. His palms poured sweat. "It was me, Dad."

"What do you mean, it was you?" his dad said, confused. "How could it be you, son?"

"I guess it was what you call an accident," Harry said.

"Well," said John Moon, his shoulders heaving, "how does an accident like this happen?"

"In the night," said Harry. "We can get in a lot of trouble at night when we think no one is looking."

While his dad sat slumped in a yard chair, Harry told him the whole story of his bleak night — his escape by ladder, his travel by train, his purchase of time magic at *Fire Magic*. To his credit, Harry stood there in his pajamas and, like a man, told him the whole sordid tale of his trip from Sleepy Hollow to Gehenna.

"I just wanted to be taller, faster," said Harry.

144

"You are not a man because you are tall, Harry. Or because you have whiskers on your chin or hair on your chest. That's just a small part of it. You are a man because you develop character," replied his father.

"Yes, Dad," said Harry.

Harry Moon looked at the damage to the MG-F — the broken dashboard, the ripped convertible cover and the nails through the fresh, saddle-soaped leather was a disaster. He felt just awful. When he looked at the pain in his dad's eyes, he felt even worse.

"Don't yes me, Harry, unless you believe it. You become a man because you do what is right. Those nine qualities that are stenciled in the kitchen, not one of them mentions sneaking around and lying to your dad and mom."

"I understand, Dad," Harry said.

Harry Cornelius Moon wasn't sure what to do. His dad seemed lost. His mom called what his dad was doing 'processing', talking out loud, trying to reach a decision.

So Harry stood in his pjs as his dad continued to 'process'. Normally, when his dad sat in his favorite white, wooden Adirondack lawn chair, he was relaxing in the backyard with an iced tea and *Motor Car* magazine. Normally, he was not moaning, looking shattered, staring up at the new sun in the sky. But then, this was anything but a normal Saturday morning.

"I don't understand, Harry, why wouldn't you just level with me? Tell me what was going on inside you. We coulda talked it out."

"I guess I thought it was kinda private, Dad."

His father looked at him and sighed.

"It was an accident, but I am at fault," Harry said. He hung his head. "I deserve to be punished."

146 "There will be a punishment, Harry. Even though I am angry, I still love you. And I do get it. When you are growing up, some stuff has to be only for you. I get that. But always remember that you and I can talk things out. That's what a dad is for, to help you figure things out."

Harry and his dad sat for awhile and discussed Harry's punishment, which was a combination of groundings and extra chores. Once again, to his credit, Harry took the punishment like a man.

In the hour that he had been awake, Harry told the truth about Friday night, discussed some of the private things with his father that had been bothering him so much. When his dad told him he was grounded for a month, Harry took it with a stiff upper lip. In just an hour on a Saturday morning, Harry did everything just about right.

Rabbit's words were true. Every prayer is answered. Just not in the way we sometimes expect a prayer to be answered. For instance, look at Harry Moon. He wanted to grow up overnight. Indeed, Harry did grow. He did not grow up in inches.

147

He grew in his ability to own his mistakes.

After breakfast, his mom said, "I am disappointed in some of these choices you made, mister."

"We all are," added Honey Moon as she chomped on a spoonful of Cheerios. She looked over at Harry with her usual smug glare. "Not surprised, of course. Just very, very disappointed." Honey waved her spoon at Harry with a flip of her wrist. "What were you thinking? You're such a blockhead sometimes."

"That will be enough, Honey," said Mary Moon.

Without needing to be told, Harry went right up to his bedroom after breakfast. He looked out the window and watched his dad yank the torn convertible top off the MG-F. Then his Dad pulled the broom from the garage and swept up the broken glass that had flown from the windshield onto the driveway.

Trapped in his room for an entire month (except, of course, for school and church), Harry hung out alone with his true self. Along the way, he even mastered the art of the one arm vanish.

As Harry thought about the goofiness of wanting to be taller and the time machine waiting to be taken apart in the garage, he also thought about Rabbit, who with his raft, had rescued a Sleepy Hollow kid from his river of sweat that was headed down some dangerous waters.

153

RABBIT TELLS THE TRUTH

Rabbit sat on the side of Harry's bed as Harry looked up at the ceiling. He was on his sixth day of being grounded. "So now you are coming to me in dreams?" asked Harry

"You never know, Harry," Rabbit said. "From time-to-time, I just might surprise you."

"You know me well, Rabbit," said Harry. "You saved me from a nightmare. Who knows what would have happened if you didn't steer that raft in the right direction."

"It's what I do. I help steer the raft."

Harry felt a smile almost as wide as the river stretch across his face. *Steer the raft, pretty cool.*

"It doesn't really matter when and how I come to you, Harry. I come. I am always with you. At the time when we first met, however, I knew you needed a Rabbit for your act so I just came to you through your friend. Sarah and I had met earlier."

"I hope she's more than a friend, Rabbit," said Harry.

"For now, she is your friend," replied Rabbit.

"A friend who kisses me from time to time."

"Two kisses," said Rabbit, "does not make it from time to time."

There it is again, thought Harry. *That whole*

darn time thing. He sat up in his bed and looked at the Harlequin Rabbit. "Why must you always bring up time?!" asked Harry in a rather big voice.

"I didn't bring it up, you did!" replied Rabbit, staring Harry down.

"Oh, sorry, Rabbit. You're right."

"Time is a funny thing," said Rabbit crinkling his nose.

161

"How is that?" asked Harry.

"It holds the magic of life," Rabbit said. "We need time to love. For example, you did not love your Mom and Dad right off the bat. You had to know them first. They diapered you and fed you and took you to the doctor for shots. Your mom took you for walks. Your dad took you for rides. You learned to trust them, to love them. You cannot rush time, for without it, you cannot love."

"You're just talking about my parents," said

Harry.

"I'm also talking about your friends," said Rabbit.

"I don't love my friends," said Harry, " I *like* my friends."

"It's a different kind of love than parent love. It's brotherly love. You may call it 'like" but it is still love in my book. When I look at you and Hao and Bailey and Declan, I see brotherly love. That, too, takes time. Time to trust, time to argue, time to agree, time to accept differences as well as similarities and be okay with that."

"I guess you are right when you say it that way," said Harry.

"And that goes for Titus Kligore too. You kinda love him, but you are still suspect of him."

"Who wouldn't be?" said Harry. "I can't stand that smelly-butt Oink."

"Harry," asked Rabbit, "do you think it can it

be easy for Titus to grow up under the roof of his father, Maximus?"

"I hadn't thought about It," Harry said.

"Well, think about it and stand in Titus's shoes for a moment. His father is ruthless, tough, and unforgiving. Maximus Kligore runs the town of Sleepy Hollow like he owns it."

"I still don't get your point," said Harry.

153

"Titus struggles to do what is right, but he has a mighty big shadow that follows him."

Harry scratched his head and looked at Rabbit. "I think I understand what you are trying to teach me."

"Oh?" said Rabbit, "what is that?"

"It is better to have a shadow that is a rabbit than a smelly dog," said Harry.

"I guess you could say it that way. But the real point is, that because you love Titus as a brother, you need to help him, despite all his troubles. That takes time. Harry, you and I can do many things, we can walk through walls, we can disappear into the great unseen, we can make the Great Elvis Gold wonder what the real magic is all about. But I tell you, Harry, nothing is more magical than life itself."

"Life isn't magical," said Harry.

"Oh, that's where you are wrong, young man," Rabbit said, shaking his head. "At the center of life is time," Rabbit continued. "Inside of life, there are seasons, time to grow, time to learn, time to plant, time to harvest, time to die. Time to love. The fullness of time is a great thing."

"Hmmmm," said Harry. "That's why you call time a funny thing?"

"Yes, sometimes it's easy to forget how magical life can be while waiting for the fullness of time."

In the quiet of being grounded, Harry had many deep and philosophical discussions with

Rabbit. It was weird for Harry because he was not allowed to watch TV, or talk on his cell, or even play video games. In the month of being grounded, there was just a silent room and he and his rabbit.

In all his thirteen years, Harry Moon had never known this quiet. Then he remembered hearing that the Great Magician would sometimes say goodbye for a while and just spend some time alone on the mountain.

With Rabbit by his side, the bedroom in the house of Nightingale Lane had become his mountain.

"Rabbit," asked Harry, "can I ask you a question because I get asked this a lot from my audience?"

"Fire away," Rabbit said as he lifted dumbbells in Harry's room.

"Rabbit, are you real?"

"O Harry, I am better than real," replied Rabbit, "I am true."

156

157

FREEDOM AND A HAIRCUT

"Time's up," John Moon said opening the door to Harry's bedroom. "And it's a beautiful Saturday morning."

Harry could hear the calm of a new day. The larks were singing. He could hear a few cars moving down Nightingale Lane.

"Dad, its weird," said Harry, as he climbed out of bed. "No one likes to be punished. But I have been thinking that you are a good guy."

"Why is that?" asked John Moon, straightening his hoodie on his Patriot's sweatshirt that Harry had given him for his thirty-fifth birthday.

"Well, I noticed when I smashed Emma, you never got red-faced and angry like, well, for instance Maximus Kligore," said Harry. "Mister Kligore practically jumps down Titus's throat when he does bad things. Mister Kligore, whoa, he is one, angry dude."

158

"Thank you, Harry. I appreciate that."

"It's weird though. I was grounded for thirty days but on the one hand, Dad, it seemed like an eternity. On the other hand, it happened in the blink of an eye," said Harry.

"Yes, I understand. I have the same sense, son," said Harry's dad.

"Hey, Dad?"

Harry's Dad moved a little further into the room. "Yes, Harry?"

"I am really sorry. For messing up your car and for lying to you and Mom."

John Moon sighed and looked out Harry's window at his car. "Thanks, Harry, I know you are."

"Do you forgive me, Dad?"

159

"I do forgive you, Harry."

"Now all you have to remember is who you are," said John.

"Who I am?"

"A boy of his word," answered John Moon.

"That's right," Harry said.

"Hey stranger, we haven't seen you in a

while," said Oscar Toledo. Oscar's smile shown brightly beneath his well groomed moustache when he saw Harry Moon come through the door of the shop.

This barber shop had been in the Toledo family since 1923 when the Toledos moved to Sleepy Hollow. It was an old-fashioned sort of place with wood floors and a neighborly, easy-going attitude. The shop even had one of those old electronic barber poles standing on the sidewalk. It was one of those gizmos that twirled red, white and blue which the Toledos had bought in the 1950s.

Harry took off his fall jacket and hung it on the hook on the wall. There were a couple of guys already getting cuts and shaves. The place was busy, but not jumping.

"Step right up," said Randy Toledo, Oscar's white-haired dad, turning an empty chair to Harry. Harry stepped up on the chair and hopped aboard. Old Man Toledo shook open a fresh white apron and fastened it with a pin around Harry's neck.

"Where have you been, Harry my man?" asked Randy.

"It's been two months since we have seen you by the look of your neck," said Thommy Toledo, the youngest of the Toledo barbers. He had a bushy red beard.

"Yeah, what happened to you?" asked Old man Toledo. He started clipping Harry's hair with his silver scissors. "Dontcha love us anymore?"

161

"I love you guys fine," Harry said. "The truth is I was grounded for a month," said Harry. He scrunched down in the chair as if to hide himself behind the apron. "I snuck out on Friday night and went to Boston and I messed up my Dad's car."

"What the heck?" asked Old Man Toledo. He moved the scissors away from Harry's ear. "You drove your dad's car?"

Harry let go a nervous chuckle. "No, nothing like that. But when I threw the escape ladder from my bedroom window, it smashed into the MG-F."

"Whoa!" said Thommy Toledo.

"What were you doin' in Boston, anyways?" asked Oscar Toledo.

"I was trying to get some magic to make me taller," said Harry.

162   "You look just fine to me," Old Man Toledo said, patting Harry on the shoulder.

"So you went to Fire Magic: All in One?" asked Oscar.

"You know it?" asked Harry, surprised.

"They do a lot of advertising," replied Oscar. "Haven't been there myself. But every time I'm in Boston, I am tempted to swing by."

"Why bother? Based on experience, it will only make you miserable," said Harry. He moaned from the recollection.

"Why be miserable?" said the voice at the end of the barber shop. Harry looked over and saw Titus Kligore in the last chair by the wall. Harry was astounded. Titus's long, slacker hair had been completely shorn. He was now sporting a buzz cut. Harry barely recognized him.

The youngest of the Toledo's, Auggie Toledo, just out of high school, took the white apron off his customer, Titus Kligore. Titus rubbed his big hand over his shaved head, grinning in Harry's direction so he could get a good look at it.

163

"You got your money's worth, that's for sure," said Auggie with a smile.

"I sure did," said Titus, with a laugh that sounded like a groan. "Hopefully, the misery will now end."

"Misery?" asked Harry. "What happened, Titus?"

"Fleas, that's what happened," said Titus.

"That stupid Oink gave me fleas. I chased him out of the house and that dog hasn't been back in over a month. He's out there somewhere. Sometimes, I look at that ugly mongrel and I don't think he is a dog at all."

Harry had to bite his tongue. "You aren't the only one."

Titus paid Auggie and then walked across the old wooden floor to Harry's chair. "I don't think he likes you, Harry Moon. Better be careful of the dark."

Titus looked at Harry. He was eye-to-eye with the kid who sat in the barber's chair. He looked at him carefully, even suspiciously. "Wait a minute, is it just me..."

"Just you?" asked Harry.

"Is it just me, or have you grown?"

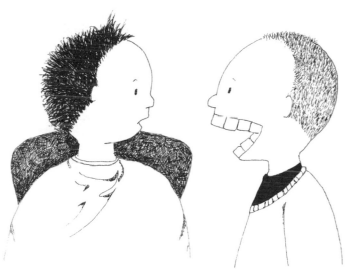

"I think he's grown, too," said Old Man Toledo.

"It's not you. It's this chair," said Harry to Titus. Old Man Toledo had played basketball in his younger days so he had to crank the chair high to get the head close to his eye line. Old Man Toledo stood six-foot-three inches. Harry glanced at his jacket on the hook. Come to think of it, this was the first time he was able to hang his jacket without standing on his tip-toes. Maybe he had grown a little and without even trying.

"No, I think your magic *is working*, Harry," said Titus as he turned to leave. "You *are growing* tall."

"Tall enough," said Harry. "Tall enough."

167

168

MARK ANDREW POE

The Adventures of Harry Moon author Mark Andrew Poe never thought about being a children's writer growing up. His dream was to love and care for animals, specifically his friends in the rabbit community.

Along the way, Mark became successful in all sorts of interesting careers. He entered the print and publishing world as a young man and his company did really, really well.

Mark became a popular and nationally sought-after health care advocate for the care and well-being of rabbits.

Years ago, Mark came up with the idea of a story about a young man with a special connection to a world of magic, all revealed through a remarkable rabbit friend. Mark worked on his idea for several years before building a collaborative creative team to help bring his idea to life. And Harry Moon was born.

In 2014, Mark began a multi-book print series project intended to launch *The Adventures of Harry Moon* into the youth marketplace as a hero defined by a love for a magic where love and 'DO NO EVIL' live. Today, Mark continues to work on the many stories of Harry Moon. He lives in suburban Chicago with his wife and his 25 rabbits.

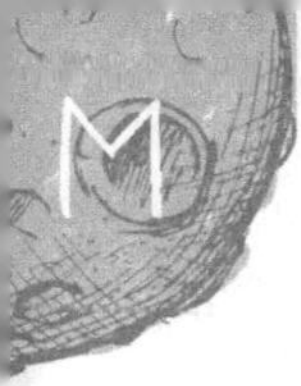
M

BE SURE TO READ THE CONTINUING AND
AMAZING ADVENTURES OF HARRY MOON

HARRY MOON  BOOK CLUB

Become a member of the
Harry Moon Book Club and receive another
of Harry's adventure every other month along
with a magician's hat full of goodies!

Hop over to **www.harrymoon.com**
and sign up today.

Kids Talk
About Harry Moon

"I think this was a great story. Mark Andrew Poe really knows how to write a good book. I could read these every day. I think Harry Moon is the best kid book I have read yet. Honestly, if you don't enjoy it, you're absolutely crazy."
                              - B. K., age 12

"Harry Moon is the best book I have ever read. I couldn't take my eyes off of it the second I started reading it! I feel sorry for Harry when he has a hard time. It feels like me. I also enjoy it because I like Sleepy Hollow. I recommend this book to people who like to laugh while they

read. You will not want to put this book down.
When you're done reading it, you may beg
your parents for all the books in the series."

- K. O., age 12

"Awesome best book ever. You should read
this. I know I did and I enjoyed it and its worth
every penny if you have a kid that is bored.
They will love this story, trust me."

- D. B., age 11

"I like Harry Moon because it tells the life of
an average eighth grader who also happens
to be an incredible magician. Again: Funniest,
best book you will ever read."

- B. D., age 12

"*The Amazing Adventures of Harry Moon* is by far was the the most fun book ever. I say this because it talks about friends and magic. Whoever reads this book will be satisfied. It's a story for all ages. Big or small. I mean, you can tell by the front cover. SO READ THIS BOOK!"

- P. L., age 11

"This is a classic book because its about a kid, a name that everyone makes fun of and the hard ships of going through middle school.
And all sisters embarrass their brothers. I think this will be a good book for kids because it shows someone who does right things."

- M. D., age 11

"I was playing with my friend Mike and I told him how good this book was. Mike paused Minecraft and asked me to why it was good without giving away the ending. I told him that it was about a kid named Harry Moon who used magic to win back his town. Now he wants to read it."

　　　　　- J. P., age 12

"I luv this book so...so...much and I think that it's one of the best books I've ever read and the story is awesome and I actually have the same problem that Harry has in this book because my friends make fun of me, too. I know how Harry feels. Anyway I loved the book and I can't wait to read the next one."

　　　　　- B. B., age 12

"I loved this book, it actually relates to problems that usually happens in a kid's mind. I love how that the author tells what the main character, Harry Moon, is thinking and his own opinions upon his own life and problems. I would definitely recommend this book to children and adults too!"

— M. R., age 12

178

"This is a good book. I would read it again just to read it. I totally recommend it. I think Mark Poe is a great author and he should make more of these books."

— T. M., age 11

"Harry Moon is a very well written book, also very humorous too! I think this is will be an AWESOME series. Great pictures. Read it!"

— K. T., age 12

"This is an epic book. Just too epic! But I am also a very fast reader, so write these books as fast as possible!"

        - R. T., age 12

"I think this is a very good book because it really expresses what it feels like to be in a kid's shoes and how they deal with life situations."

        - A. L., age 12

179

"Harry Moon has great twists and teaches a lesson that I might need one day. I am only eleven but this book helped me think about a few challenges I might run into and this book taught me how important friends and family are and that's what helped me the most I

loved this book and I think other kids my age or older will love this book. Have to find a rabbit."
> – P. R., age 11

"I liked Harry Moon because the author had a great idea of telling about a kid who gets humiliated in middle school and because it's funny.
> – T. B., age 12

180

I loved Harry Moon. You hooked me. I loved it. p.s. Please write more books."
> – N. L., age 12

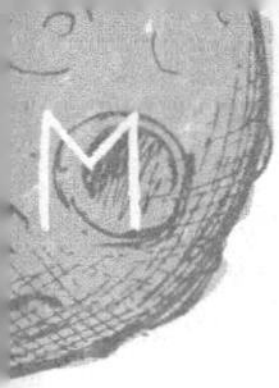
M

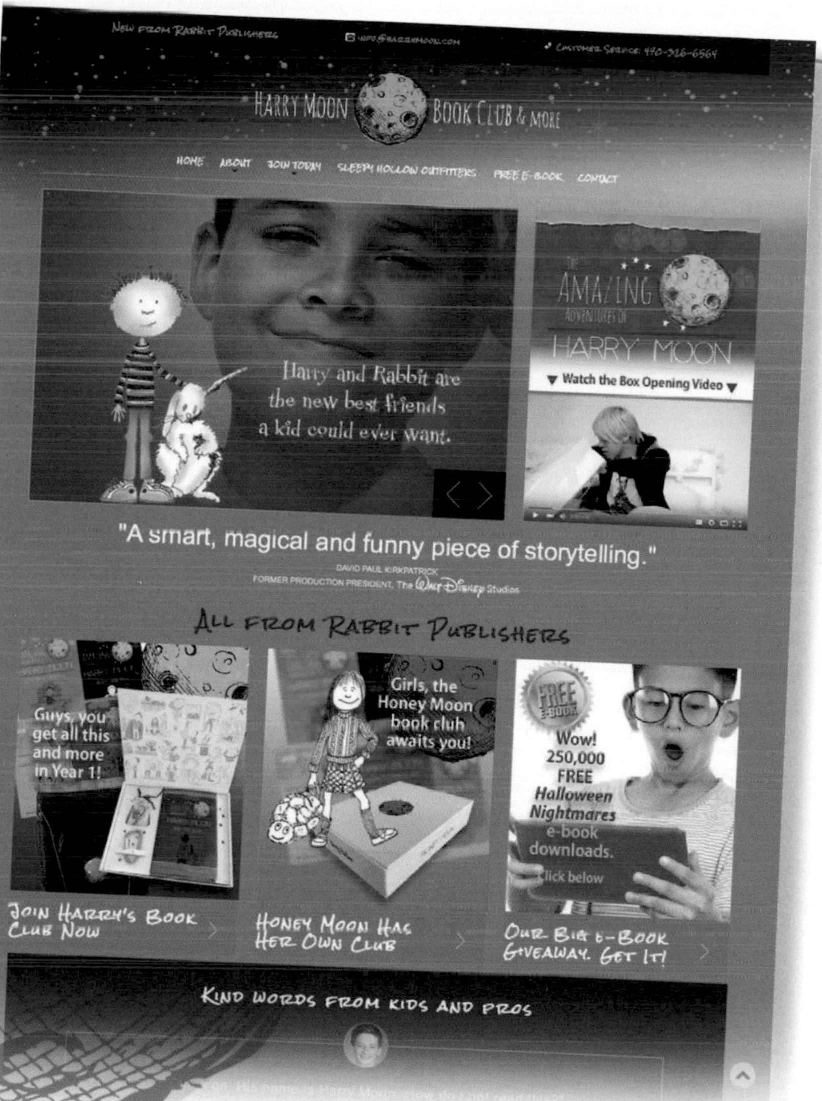
New from Rabbit Publishers
info@harrymoon.com
Customer Service: 470-326-6564
Harry Moon Book Club & more
Home About Join Today Sleepy Hollow Outfitters Free E-Book Contact
Harry and Rabbit are the new best friends a kid could ever want.
The Amazing Adventures of Harry Moon
▼ Watch the Box Opening Video ▼
"A smart, magical and funny piece of storytelling."
DAVID PAUL KIRKPATRICK
FORMER PRODUCTION PRESIDENT, The Walt Disney Studios
All from Rabbit Publishers
Guys, you get all this and more in Year 1!
Girls, the Honey Moon book club awaits you!
FREE E-BOOK
Wow! 250,000 FREE Halloween Nightmares e-book downloads.
Join Harry's Book Club Now
Honey Moon Has Her Own Club
Our Big E-Book Giveaway. Get It!
Kind words from kids and pros

Visit HARRYMOON.COM for everything Harry, Honey & the latest news

VISIT HARRYMOON.COM FOR
EVERYTHING HARRY, HONEY & THE LATEST NEWS

Every 12 month subscriber receives each of these benefits:

1. **SIX hardcover editions** of *The Amazing Adventures of Harry Moon*. That's a new book delivered every two months. *(3 books for 6 mo. subscribers)*

2. **SIX free e-book versions** of each new book (downloaded using our included Harry Moon smart phone and tablet app. *(3 books for 6 mo. subscribers)*

3. Your first book is delivered in a beautiful **Harry Moon "cigar style" Collectables Box**.

4. **Wall posters** of Harry, Rabbit and all their friends are on the inside of each book's dust jacket—images straight from the Sleepy Hollow Portrait Gallery.

5. The very popular and useful **monogramed drawstring backpack** from the Sleepy Hollow Outfitters store.

6. From the Sleepy Hollow Magic Store a **pouch of magical fragrances** transporting you to the town's aromas.

7. The large 15" x 21" **Fun Map of Sleepy Hollow**—takes you everywhere around town.

9. A **special edition** of the *Sleepy Hollow Gazette*, including a welcome from the mayor and stories about the upcoming books and not-to-miss events. PLUS, you receive monthly editions of the *Sleepy Hollor Gazette* via email and the app.

9. Plus, if you choose, the Keepsake Box will also include the **golden Sleepy Hollow Outfitters carabiner**. Very handy.

10. And a second optional choice is to include the very cool **Harry Moon monogramed knit beanie**.

Total value of this package - $215 (plus optional items 9 and 10)

Get your gear where Harry Moon shops!

Popular Sleepy Hollow Apparel, Accessories & Books

Color "Friend" T-Shirt

$20

T-shirt is fabric laundered, 4.3 oz., 60/40 combed ringspun cotton/polyester. Made in America. Available in one Kid Size: L, and in Adult Sizes: S, M, L, and XL.
ADD TO CART

Olive "Friend" T-Shirt

$20

T-shirt is fabric laundered, 4.3 oz., 60/40 combed ringspun cotton/polyester. Made in America. Available in one Kid Size: L, and in Adult Sizes: S, M, L, and XL.
ADD TO CART

Black "Friend" T-Shirt

$20

T-shirt is fabric laundered, 4.3 oz., 60/40 combed ringspun cotton/polyester. Made in America. Available in one Kid Size: L, and in Adult Sizes: S, M, L, and XL.
ADD TO CART

Grey "Do No Evil" T-Shirt

$20

T-shirt is fabric laundered, 4.3 oz., 60/40 combed ringspun cotton/polyester. Made in America. Available in one Kid Size: L, and in Adult Sizes: S, M, L, and XL.
ADD TO CART

Black "Do No Evil" T-Shirt

$20

T-shirt is fabric laundered, 4.3 oz., 60/40 combed ringspun cotton/polyester. Made in America. Available in one Kid Size: L, and in Adult Sizes: S, M, L, and XL.
ADD TO CART

Harry Moon Knit Beanie

$12

This stretchy knit cap is 8" high and 8" wide. Made from 100% acrylic yarn, it features Harry's iconic "moon" logo on a sewn on tag.
ADD TO CART

Sleepy Hollow Outfitters Gold Carabiner

$5

It's a fun, 3" long metal carabiner, handy for carrying keys and for many other uses. (Not for actual climbing.)
ADD TO CART

Halloween Nightmares

WHITE BOOK SERIES

Red cover $15   E-Book $9

While others are trick-or-treating, eighth grade wizard Harry Moon is flying on... past severed hands, ...yard witching rituals in ...weaving a decade old curse at the annual Sleepy Hollow Halloween Bonfire. ...are in for the fight
ADD TO CART; ...FREE E-BOOK

Sleepy Hollow OUTFITTERS
Est. 1675

Books below available by joining Harry's Book Club?

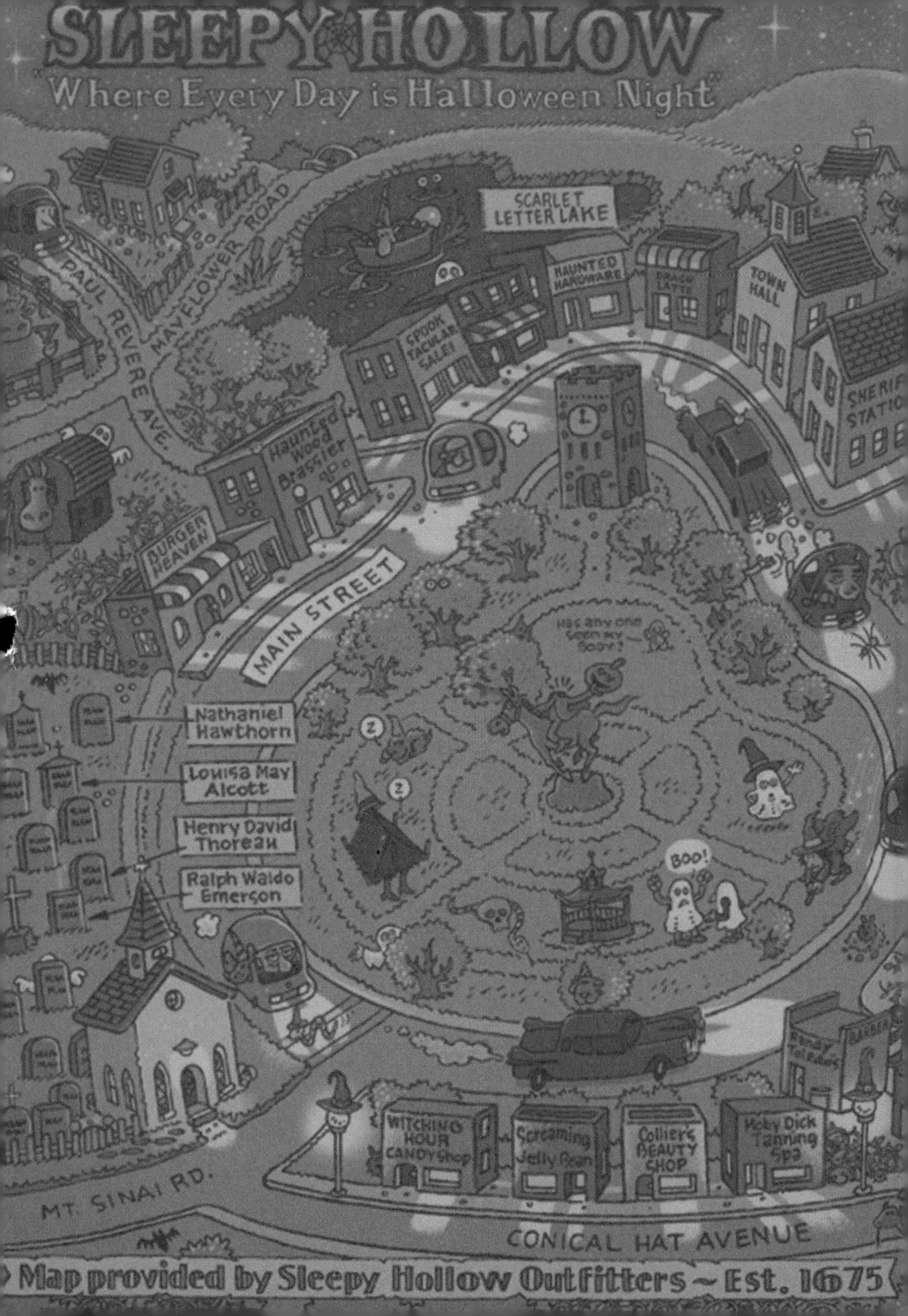
SLEEPY HOLLOW
"Where Every Day is Halloween Night"
SCARLET LETTER LAKE
MAYFLOWER ROAD
PAUL REVERE AVE.
HAUNTED HARDWARE
TOWN HALL
SHERIF STATIO
SPOOK TACULAR SALE!
Haunted Wood Brassier
BURGER HEAVEN
MAIN STREET
Has any one seen my Body?
Nathaniel Hawthorn
Louisa May Alcott
Henry David Thoreau
Ralph Waldo Emerson
BOO!
WITCHING HOUR CANDY Shop
Screaming Jelly Bean
Collier's BEAUTY SHOP
Moby Dick Tanning Spa
MT. SINAI RD.
CONICAL HAT AVENUE
Map provided by Sleepy Hollow Outfitters ~ Est. 1675